WHAT PEOPLE ARE SAYING ABOUT

THE VIBRANT EMERITUS

It was my very great pleasure reading *The Vibrant Emeritus*. Once I got started, I couldn't put it down. By the time I finished, I knew we were brothers.

The Vibrant Emeritus is a book for those considering the path of the Enlightened Elder. Becoming an Elder is not an easy path, but the work – if followed sincerely – will transform your life and the lives of those you love and serve. This is an authentic and powerful book because Richard Stuecker gets it! He did this work for himself and he knows the way. With so much to teach, his book will become an ever-deepening experience of your own initiation into the mature masculinity. Be sure to read it several times!

John C. Robinson, author, *Bedtime Stories for Elders: What Fairy Tales Can Teach Us About the New Aging* and *What Aging Men Want: The Odyssey as a Parable of Male Aging*

T0168979

The Vibrant Emeritus

The Elder in the Twenty-First Century

The
Vibrant Emeritus

The Elder in the Twenty-First Century

Richard Stuecker

BOOKS

Winchester, UK
Washington, USA

First published by O-Books, 2014
O-Books is an imprint of John Hunt Publishing Ltd., Laurel House, Station Approach,
Alresford, Hants, SO24 9JH, UK
office1@jhpbooks.net
www.johnhuntpublishing.com

For distributor details and how to order please visit the 'Ordering' section on our website.

Text copyright: Richard Stuecker 2013

ISBN: 978 1 78279 589 6

A CIP catalogue record for this book is available from the British Library.

Design: Lee Nash

Printed and bound by CPI Group (UK) Ltd, Croydon, CR0 4YY

We operate a distinctive and ethical publishing philosophy in all
areas of our business, from our global network of authors to
production and worldwide distribution.

CONTENTS

Acknowledgements

This work would not be possible without the following people who totally enrich my life with joy, hope and wisdom.

Barbara, my wife, who encourages my every project and puts up with the isolating nature of my work.

Allan Podbelsek, my mentor who as an elder lives the way of the Vibrant Emeritus.

Tim Schladand, my training partner who has initiated hundreds of men across the country and across the seas. He inspires in me boundless creativity, confidence and bodacious living.

Ronnie Hager, a brilliant young man whose friendship, search for manhood, leadership, and fatherhood inspires in me the best Elder qualities of blessing, mentoring and inspiring.

And the men who mentored me at crucial times in my life: **John Clum**, **Frank Cayce**, **Leon Hisle**, and **Wayne Hunnicutt**.

Introduction

The Time of the Seven Tasks of the Vibrant Emeritus

I come to a place in the road. It is late and the weather is changing. I come to a place known as the Time of the Seven Tasks. I ask myself: Where have I been? What have I done? What have I learned? What have I collected? Do I need more? Who loves me? Whom do I love?

This is the first task.

I come to a place in the road where the shadows are long and dark. I ask myself: What is the mask I wear? As a Lover? As a Warrior? As a Magician? As a King? What masks must I shed?

This is the second task.

I come to a crossroads. It is late and I am chilly. Which road will I choose? What will I need for the road? Am I enough?

This is the third task.

I come to a clearing. I sit upon the ground and look deeply into the sky. I remember looking up at the sky as a youth. I had such dreams! I was inspired! Can I return to those golden dreams? Can I make them real with what I now know?

This is the fourth task.

I come to a turn in the road. I look around me. The world is splendid! The world is animated with color and vibrant life! My spirit flies!

This is the fifth task.

I come to place in the road where I feel within myself a noble challenge. I ask myself: What will I give? What will I create? Whom will I serve? Whom will I mentor? What is my legacy?

This is the sixth task.

I come to stopping place. The view ahead is dim. It is time to rest. I ask myself: Am I fulfilled? Can I let go? Will I find peace?

These are the Seven Tasks of the Vibrant Emeritus.

Purpose

This is a book about becoming a vital and generative Elder: a *Vibrant Emeritus*, one who serves the community in the twenty-first century with wisdom, creativity, and blessing. One who mentors the next generation. One who readies himself for death and creates a legacy.

It is a book for men 50 years of age or older who are feeling the natural pull to let go of one's first journey in life and to embrace one's second. It is for men who are drawn to taking stock of where they are in life: men who wonder about their life after the time when child-rearing, career-building, and collecting objects might transform into a time of deeper spirituality, a new purpose, a kind of grace, and a new vibrancy about one's life. This transformation toward an abundant point of view, toward wisdom, and toward giving back to one's community takes some work.

The purpose of this book is to support men taking this challenge. It is a path that can lead to deeper spirituality, renewed energy, and a life-affirming consciousness. It can lead to a time where one connects one's youthful dreams, aspirations and values, with the knowledge, skills and acumen one has acquired over a lifetime to forge one's final life challenge and purpose. It means evaluating one's life achievements, losses, gains, wounds, and motivation so far. It can include confronting one's shadows, especially those regarding aging. It takes blending the innocence, values, aspirations and vision for oneself, the community one once held as a youth with one's sagacity. It can be a blissful journey and one's life can become a time of abundance, fulfillment and personal satisfaction as one builds one's legacy.

For many men, aging can be a difficult struggle. Even thinking about getting older can be daunting, even frightening if one sees it only as only a time of diminishing health and capacity; a life formerly fulfilled by raising a family, building a career, and acquiring possessions that now might seem empty; a letting go of one's personal definitions as a worker, an achiever; or a time of life that becomes a series of disappointments. Often, when I talk with men in their fifties and early sixties, I find an immediate resistance to thinking about, much less, accepting aging. Over and over they say to me: "I'm not ready to look at that yet!"

Certainly, in a culture that appears so centered on youth and finding ways to stay young, on competition with winners and losers, on seeking achievements and accolades, on rushing to more and more experiences, it is understandable that many men are confused and reluctant to put their energy toward a new approach to aging. Ours is not often a culture that honors Elders, seeks the sagacious, or has maintained rites of passage for men entering what can be a new, enticing and enriching stage of life. The vast changes that have come since the Industrial Revolution have robbed our culture of connection with the community, unity with nature, and celebration and acceptance of all the seasons of our life cycle. We no longer have meaningful rites of passage for many of life's transformations including aging.

I have come to believe that these disconnections affect our culture and our psyches for the worse. Creating and developing twenty-first century renewals of rituals, celebrations, support from others in our neighborhoods and community, seem to be crucial to bringing cultural and individual health to ourselves, our families, and to our community. Recently there has been a revival of these institutions in many places in an attempt to give meaning to passages from adolescence into manhood and womanhood. These include initiation rituals, vision quests, and other initiatory experiences. The men's movement has grown new ways of initiating men from youth to an adulthood that is marked by integrity, responsibility and a definitive mission.

Yet, within our culture and heritage, sources exist for our renewal. These sources lie in the myths, legends and folklore of our ancestors. They can be found in the work of a number of researchers, social philosophers, anthropologists, and psychologists have studied them and who have suggested that men aging can embrace this time of life with a conscious purpose, celebration, giving, mentoring and fully experiencing one's life even unto death.

Our challenge is not to repeat the rites and rituals of our past or copy them, but to recreate them in the vernacular that speaks to us and inspires us in the twenty-first century. Based on my understanding of the lore, research, and study of the work of Jungian psychologists, folklorists, storytellers, social philosophers and cultural anthropologists listed in the references section of this book I have organized each chapter on the Legend of Parsifal and on seven challenges or tasks listed below:

1. Assessing the Journey So Far
2. Confronting One's Shadows
3. Standing at the Crossroads
4. Becoming Generative
5. Deepening Spirituality
6. Mentoring the Next Generation
7. Embracing Death

Context

Your heart has been beating since you were in your mother's womb. It will beat until you take your last breath. Place your hand on your heart. Can you feel your heart beating? Can you feel the pulse deep in your heart? Can you remember how your heart beat when you were young? After a race or a challenge? When you experienced something thrilling? When you first fell in love? When you dreamed deep dreams for yourself? When you yearned to fulfill the vision of your youthful heart?

Are you listening to your heart now? Do you feel a deep calling to fulfill your youthful dreams now that you have bravely gained knowledge, skill and wisdom in the adventures of your life? Do you feel a call to be vibrant as you age? Are you ready for a new purpose in your life? Are you ready to serve? to generate? to create? to teach? to mentor? to heal? to bless?

Are you ready to become a Vibrant Emeritus?

Or do you find fear? The fear of limited capacity? The fear of loss of control? The fear of death?

Perhaps, as you listen to your heart, you will find both.

There is a difference in what one aging man has called "the Way of the Old Geezer" and the "Way of the Vibrant Emeritus." The choice is yours.

Choosing the Way of the Vibrant Emeritus is often difficult for men living in the post-industrial twenty-first century where the path to eminent elderhood is difficult to find, where role models are rare, and where elders are often ignored, put aside and discredited.

In the thousands of years that we have memory, tradition and written history, we know that as men aged in society in former ages they often were honored, sought out for advice, and were charged with transferring the wisdom, lore and tradition of the community to the young. The elders initiated young men as full members of the tribe. They were honored not for simply growing old. They were honored because they transformed the knowledge, skill and experience they gained from living into wisdom, council and vision. They were the keepers of the community's heritage, collective knowledge, and traditions. They were the healers, teachers, initiators, counselors, storytellers, and vessels of the culture's lore.

The industrial age changed how we perceive ourselves, how we live and survive in a world, and how we view aging men. We have moved to the cities, worked in factories and businesses removed from Nature, and focused on earning money and collecting objects. Aging men no longer pass down skills, knowledge and the acumen to survive to the young. Many of us have abandoned our neighborhoods, isolated ourselves from others, and frequently lost our connection to community. Within these changes, the role of elder has been diminished and even forgotten.

At the same time, life spans have increased so that by age fifty we are looking at twenty, thirty, forty and even more years of vibrancy. For some this might mean a life of leisure with travel, sports or some other special interests. Others might choose to consult regarding their former professions, work part time or even pursue a second career. Unfortunately, others might give up, resigned to a life of dismal diminishment.

The Vibrant Emeritus integrates travel and leisure, reduced workloads and special interests with a life of new purpose, deeper spirituality, giving of one's abundance, and mentoring younger men and women. These men become honored Elders, Vibrant Emeriti.

The vision and consciousness of the Vibrant Emeritus is one that looks outward toward the community and centers on building one's legacy gifted to those who come after him. The key question is the question Parsifal asks the second time he enters the Grail Castle, after a life of heroic adventures: "Whom do you serve?" Once Parsifal asks this question the wasteland blooms and transforms into verdant abundance. The Vibrant Emeritus takes on the challenge of renewing the world from a place of generativity, creativity and spirituality focused on serving others.

At last, he embraces death as the next great adventure of his life.

Major Sources

Angeles Arrien

I have been using Angeles Arrien's work as a source for my own transformative experiences, workshops, trainings, and retreats. Arrien was an internationally honored cultural anthropologist.

She had spoken at conferences I had the honor to design, organize and manage.

I have used three specific works as sources for this book. *Signs of Life* (1998), the CD course *The Second Half of Life: The Blossoming of Your Creative Self* (1997) and the book, *The Second Half of Life: Opening the Eight Gates of Wisdom* (2005). I found especially useful her initiatory eight gates for men and women embracing their roles as Elders. These include:

1. The Silver Gate: Facing new experiences and the unknown
2. The White Picket Gate: Changing identities, discovering one's true face
3. The Clay Gate: Intimacy, Sensuality and Sexuality
4. The Black and White Gate: Relationships: the crucible of love, generosity, betrayal and forgiveness
5. The Rustic Gate: Creativity, Service and Generativity
6. The Bone Gate: Authenticity, Character and Wisdom
7. The Natural Gate: The Presence of Grace: Happiness, Satisfaction, and Peace
8. The Gold Gate: Nonattachment, Surrender and Letting Go

Allan B. Chinen

Another primary source for this book is Allan Chinen's work *In the Ever After: Fairy Tales and the Second Half of Life* (1992). The short biography on his website reads:

Allan B. Chinen, MD is a Clinical Professor of Psychology at the University of California, San Francisco and in private practice in San Francisco. He has lectured extensively and presented numerous workshops on the role of myths, fairy tales and legends on our life stories – the scripts we live out.

Chinen has read, analyzed and interpreted more than 4,000 Elder Tales. This study led him to arrange what he finds to be the seven essential tasks men must take on in order to be fully actualized as a generative elder. These tasks include to:

1. Deal with the specter of the losses of aging and use one's assets from life's experiences to grow;
2. Confront one's shadows, move to consciousness of empathy for others;
3. Return to the transcendent goals and values from one's youth;
4. Become generative;
5. Integrate the childhood's innocence with the sagacity of maturity;
6. Deepen one's spirituality by connecting with wonder and delight in life;
7. Inspire and mentor the next generation.

Michael Gurian

It has been my pleasure to know and work with the *New York Times* best-selling author of such important books as *The Wonder of Boys*, *A Fine Young Man* and *Boys and Girls Learn Differently*. He has entered his own 'second journey' and following a debilitating illness he has turned his attention as a social philosopher and interpreter of recent scientific findings to aging in his new book, *The Wonder of Aging*. In this book Michael presents a holistic paradigm that includes three stages: the Age of Transformation, the Age of Distinction, and the Age of Completion. His work provides this book with its scientific and philosophic underpinnings.

Michael Meade

Michael Meade, DHL is a renowned storyteller, author, folklorist, and scholar of mythology, anthropology, and psychology. He combines his spellbinding skills of storytelling with a deep understanding of ancient myths, legends and folktales, and a highly insightful knowledge of cross-cultural rituals. He has an unusual ability to distill and synthesize these disciplines especially in his book *Men and the Water of Life: Initiation and the Tempering of Men* (1993). Part five of that work addresses the last stage of life. It is inspiring and provides a deep understanding of Elder initiation.

John C. Robinson

John Robinson is a Jungian psychologist and author. Concerning initiation into the Elder Journey he writes: "[When] I started to age, I sensed that growing older continues this same unfolding transformation of consciousness that had begun with midlife. More than that, I realized that aging itself offers the highest levels of spiritual realization if we understand and surrender to its powerful energies."

Three of his books I found especially enlightening and their concepts underlie my thinking: *Death of a Hero, Birth of the Soul* (1995), *The Three Secrets of Aging: A Radical Guide* (2012), and *What Aging Men Want: The Odyssey as a Parable of Men Aging* (2013).

Richard Rohr

Father Richard Rohr is the founder of the Center for Action and Contemplation that sponsors powerful initiatory workshops and experiences for men. He is a Franciscan priest who grounds his work in the Franciscan Alternative orthodoxy that practices contemplation and compassion. He has written a number of insightful and inspirational works. For this book, *Falling Upward: A Spirituality for the Two Halves of Life* (2011) and *Quest for the Grail* (1994) were extremely helpful, especially Rohr's explication of the meaning of the Parsifal legend and its symbols.

Zalman Schachter-Shalomi and Ronald S. Miller

Schachter-Shalomi and Miller are the authors of the groundbreaking *From Age-ing to Sage-ing: A Profound New Vision of*

Growing Older (1995). They divide their understanding of conscious aging into three sections: the Theory of Spiritual Eldering; Spiritual Eldering and Personal Transformation; and Spiritual Eldering and Social Transformation. In the introduction, Schachter-Shalomi writes:

> In putting forth a new model of spiritual Elderhood, I am not only reviving an ancient and venerable institution that has enriched civilization since time immemorial, but taking it a step further. As part of the emerging approach to late-life development, the contemporary sage draws on three sources: models of the traditional tribal Elder whose wisdom guided the social order for thousands of years; state-of-the-art break-throughs in brain-mind and consciousness research; and the ecology movement, which urges us to live in harmony with the natural world. These forces converge in the sage, whose explorations in consciousness are giving birth to an Elderhood that is appropriate for the modern world.

Structure

The Seven Tasks of the Vibrant Emeritus that provide the structure of this book also form a mandala of the personality in one's Elder years. While each task is given sequentially as one expands one's vision and transforms into a Vibrant Emeritus, the tasks also emerge over and over and challenge one, as one goes deeper and deeper into one's authenticity, spirituality, and gener-ativity. With each challenge one attempts to let go until one reaches a time and place of one's ultimate letting go: death.

This book begins with a retelling and a discussion of the Legend of Parsifal, of the grail legends. It is my opinion that Parsifal embodies the complete journey of the Vibrant Emeritus in that:

1. It begins with Parsifal's rearing by his mother, Heart's Sorrow, in a deep wilderness as an innocent and naif; continues with his awakening to his manhood and battle with his shadow, the Red Knight; narrates the story of a young man who connects with a mentor, Gournamond;
2. Tells of his heroic Warrior years as he quests for the grail, forgets his quest and finally, as he ages, remembers his purpose and once again enters the Grail Castle, and asks the transformative question "Whom do you serve?";
3. Describes his ascendency as Grail King who rules with blessing, an abundant heart and compassion: the embodiment of the Vibrant Emeritus.

Following the Parsifal legend, seven chapters focus on each of the Seven Tasks of the Transcendent Elder. Each chapter is an invitation to consider the task, be inspired by a classic tale, and consider a contemporary story that represents the task. It invites the reader to take on challenges to work with a specific task and to develop a practice so that one might deepen and broaden one's life as a Vibrant Emeritus. Therefore, this book is a guidebook and a workbook for men who wish to explore consciously their second journey in life.

How To Use This Book

This book is intended as a tool men might use to consciously embrace their vibrancy in the emeritus years of their lives. If one has attended the life-changing Vibrant Emeritus Initiation sponsored by the Vibrant Emeritus Center founded by the author, it can be a valuable follow-up to the rite-of-passage experience encountered there. For men who are encountering these concepts for the first time and who want to do the activities, it is highly recommended that one work with a partner or with a small group of men that supports the learning and the practices described.

The Seven Tasks form a journey of sorts, but they are not a checklist one ticks off as completed; but offers a practice as one encounters over and over the challenges of deepening one's vibrancy, consciousness and compassion. One might want to move chapter by chapter using this book as a guide. Or, one might select a chapter that might be especially useful to one at a particular time or challenge in one's life as an aging man.

The classic tales are presented to help connect one to one's interior archetypal self. Each classic tale presents several archetypes of the Elder and each tale illuminates one of the tasks of the Vibrant Emeritus. The contemporary stories present a twenty-first century context that the reader might find useful in connecting each task to one's own life. The recommendation is to reflect on each story or tale and to construct a tale based on one's own life to enrich one's experience with the task.

Finally, this book is based on the resources described above and others listed at the end. Exploring these sources might provide new insights not provided here.

Chapter 1

Parsifal:
The Journey of the Vibrant Emeritus

The grail legend of Parsifal, summarized below, presents the journey of the Vibrant Emeritus in its totality. That is, having completed a hero's journey, Parsifal reenters the Grail Castle and encounters once more the opportunity that he had envisioned as a youth but had been too naive to accomplish; which is to ask the crucial grail question: "Whom do you serve?" Asking this question heals the wounded Fisher King, restores the wasted kingdom to its verdant glory and transforms him into the Grail King initiating a reign of justice and prosperity. As each of us comes to terms with the ending of our Hero life, we have an opportunity to honor our life journey so far, let it go, re-encounter our youthful values, virtues and visions, and enter a new time in our lives of mentoring and blessing. As Parsifal protects, blesses, and mentors as the abundant, loving and vibrant Grail King, so too do we have the opportunity to enter new consciousness acting from our own wise and loving Elder energy.

Unlike the Aging Hero, the Vibrant Emeritus takes stock of his life of achievements and accolades, honors them, places them in his trophy case and moves into a time in his life that is equally challenging and vital. The Vibrant Emeritus consciously embraces the last half of one's life with energy and direction, this time to impart what one has learned, skills one has gained, and values one has embraced. One is now ready to take up again the vision of his youth that might once have been seen as impractical or undoable. One is ready to mentor the next generation. It is a time of letting go and letting go and letting go as one moves toward greater and greater simplicity of means and purpose, getting ready for the ultimate act of surrender: death.

This is quite often a difficult task for many men.

Our culture seems to embrace a youth-focused culture, esteems heroic achievement, and frequently perceives aging and the Elder years as years of diminished capacity rather than a time of increased wisdom and graceful completion. Many men have a tendency to hold onto possessions and positions, often refusing to enable younger men to take their rightful place within corporations and organizations, sometimes waiting until they are pushed out or let go against their will. Others escape to the golf course, cruises, vacations, hobbies and, sometimes, addictions.

Continuing to advise, consult or continue to be a more limited part of a business is often an ideal way to leave one's career. Rewarding oneself for a life well lived is an honorable way to enter one's retirement. The key question of how one might live one's second journey is, however, a question of how might one accept and change one's consciousness from acquiring and achieving or an inward and personal focus to a viewpoint of supporting the success of others, mentoring those who might benefit from one's acumen, and blessing with positivity those who come after us.

The Vibrant Emeritus is one who lets go and consciously embraces a life of deeper connection with spirituality, with one's true purpose in life, with blessing one's family, friends and colleagues, with empowering and mentoring younger men and women and with living a rich life of giving that ends with the final release of one's life and entering one's next great adventure.

Parsifal's life is the story of a youth raised by a mother who seeks to keep him from living the adventure of his masculine life. Inspired by a vision of five glorious knights, he seeks the life lived by his father and brothers. Uneducated and naive, he leaves the forest (a symbol of the unconscious and the magical) and enters the world of men. He finds a mentor, a Vibrant Emeritus, who leads him to his heroic, adventurous, yet deeply spiritual mission: to heal the Fisher King and, thus, heal the land, bringing it back to abundance and life-healing energy. Encountering his noble mission before he has lived his heroic life, he fails to ask the crucial question we all must ask ourselves if we are to transform ourselves in our second half of life as a vibrant, vital, and ennobling Elder: "Whom do you serve?" Following a noble life of heroic adventures, Parsifal reenters the Grail Castle and finally asks the transformative question. Immediately, the anguished Fisher King is healed; the wasteland blooms with abundance and bounty; and Parsifal is installed in his full manhood as Grail King: the King who rules with vision, blessing, giving, generativity, and wise mentoring.

The Legend of Parsifal

Part 1

Once upon a time, in a time long ago, in a time dimly remembered, in a time when legends lived in the loaming, in a deep forest at the edge of where men lived, a nameless child was raised by his mother. Her name was Heart's Sorrow.

Heart's Sorrow was the wife of a great and noble knight. On the night before his final battle, he loved Heart's Sorrow with the fierce love of a man departing for war. All night they loved and in the early morning, her hair and body entangled in her lover's body, she whispered: "You have made a boy child inside me." They both wept with joy.

She wept again with pride at the sight of her husband and her strong sons, their armor shining under the morning sun, giving them the aura of demigods. They were the knights of the King, the protectors of the kingdom.

As women have suffered in quiet silence and loneliness and fear when their men went off to war, Heart's Sorrow also suffered, but her suffering was abated by the child growing inside her. She prepared herself and her home for his birth. Months passed but no word came about the war or her husband

and sons. One morning, a lone messenger came to her home. The mournful clip-clop of the messenger's horse proclaimed the sad news before his doleful knock at the door. The lady crumpled to the floor in anguish when the messenger confirmed what she knew: her husband and sons would never return.

"Never! Never shall this unborn son of mine know anything of this world of woe and misery. He will never know of this so-called civilized world, the ways of knights and kings, or the arts of war."

At midnight, the son was born into the world. In the morning, Heart's Sorrow closed the door of her home and, taking the newborn, walked deep into the forest as far as she could travel and be sure that no men would ever find her hut.

Heart's Sorrow taught the boy nothing of his father and brothers, nothing of the world she had abandoned, nothing of the knowledge of heroes she kept deep inside her. Now an only child, the boy wore homespun clothes, and grew up uneducated, simple and innocent.

The forest was thick and teeming with life and full of mystery. He connected deeply with its verdant life, knew many types of trees, the use of plants, and formed a deep connection with all living animals. He grew naturally strong and, as he moved out of childhood, a deep longing grew in his heart. But knowing nothing of life outside of his mother's hut and the forest, his heart stayed restless.

One day, the boy was chasing squirrels close to where the forest ended. He saw an amazing light flickering in the leaves like the sun on a summer's day. But the sun was behind him. He drew closer and closer to the light and at last found its source. Riding high on massive steeds in full armor and regalia rode five of the King's knights. He fell back, struck to the ground by their magnificence.

"They must be gods!" he thought.

The young man raced back to his mother's hut.

"Who were these visions?"

"They are knights, my son. I had hoped that this day would never have come. But deep in my heart I knew it would."

"Tell me, Mother! Tell me everything about them!"

"I brought you to this place to keep you safe and secure. Your father was once a knight in service to the King as these men are. So, too, were your brothers. And what did they bring me but sadness and unending pain. Beautiful men cut down by their own wild desires. I swore this would never happen to you."

"But, Mother, I feel something deep inside me! I want to follow them and become one of them!"

"Yes, I know, my beloved son. It is in your blood and your blood boils to be like your father. That is his legacy to you."

She sighed deeply. "And this is mine. I give you this homespun garment to wear under your knightly garb. And this advice: 'Respect women and do not ask too many questions.'"

The boy departed at once, his heart beating, into a new life for which he had no preparation, knowledge, or cunning.

Questions you might ask yourself:

Youth is a time before one makes a name for oneself. Parsifal is protected by his mother and kept simple and uneducated. How do you remember your mother's involvement in your life as a youth?

Parsifal's father is dead. How do you remember your father's involvement in your life?

Parsifal is kept simple and ignorant of the ways of the world. How ready did you feel you were to become a man when you were a young man?

Parsifal is dazzled by the knights whose armor and weapons inspire him to go claim his manhood as a knight. Were you dazzled by any men who represented manhood to you?

Parsifal's mother gave him two pieces of advice that influenced his life. What legacies did you receive from your birth family that have influenced your life?

Part 2

In his travels pursuing the knights, he came across a magnificent tent. He had never seen one. "It is a divine cathedral!" he thought, and he thought he might be nourished for all of his life if he entered. He imagined it was built for God. He fell to his knees in supplication and prayer.

Within, he found a maiden and a great banquet lain out. He knew he had found paradise. After a wondrous meal he took a talisman from the damsel. She was to be his inspiration for life. The maiden begged him to leave, as her knight was returning and he would kill the still nameless man.

He continued to search for the five knights, seeking information from everyone he met, asking directions and inquiring about how he might become a knight.

"You must go to the court of the King," they told him. And they laughed in his face, such a bumpkin in homespun garb seeking knighthood. "You must do noble deeds, acts of valor, great feats of manhood to become one of the King's knights. What chance do you have?"

But he persisted going from place to place, town to town, until he arrived at the King's palace. There he was taken to the King as a joke, an entertainment for the court. But the King did not laugh. He said: "Boy, you must learn many things, manly and knightly things to be dubbed a knight by a king."

At the court was a damsel who had not laughed in six years. It was said that when she laughed again, it would be because she had witnessed the arrival of the best knight in the world. Seeing the young man dressed in homespun garment, clearly uneducated, and surely innocent, she bust into joyful laughter.

The King wondered out loud: "Is this truly the best knight in the entire world?" He dubbed him on the spot.

"I demand of you, my King, the armor and steed of the Red Knight!" The Red Knight was the most dangerous and infamous of knights in the land. Again the court knights burst into amazed laughter. The King simply replied, "They are yours, if you can get them!"

Upon leaving the court, the young man met the Red Knight. His heart stopped for a moment at the resplendent sight. But then he said, "I will have your armor, Red Knight! I will fight you to the death!"

The Red Knight smirked at this young man in homespun clothing, armed with a dagger.

"Yes, you may have it, if you can get it!"

With that the Red Knight readied himself for battle with his sword and lance. He moved into position to run down this arrogant boy. He charged and knocked down the young man. Leaving his horse, the Red Knight stood over him ready for the kill. But the young man threw his dagger, piercing the Red Knight's eye. Like a magnificent statue falling, the Red Knight crumpled to the ground, dead. The young man vowed he would never take another life. Instead, when he defeated a man, he sent him to the King to swear fealty.

The young man took the Red Knight's armor and horse, but he had no idea how to put the armor on. The Red Knight's page helped him, and he tried to convince him to let go of his homespun clothing. But the young man clung to the garments his mother had given him. He wore the homespun tunic beneath his armor and rode away.

On his journey, he met a mentor, Gournamond. "Teach me the ways of manhood," the young man asked. "Help me to find my mission." All that a father might teach his son, Gournamond taught the young man. It took many months. These were the most important teachings of his godfather:

Never seduce or be seduced by a maiden.

You must search for the Grail Castle with all your might.

When you reach the Grail Castle, you must ask this question: "Whom does the Grail serve?"

Questions you might ask yourself:

Parsifal enters the tent of a maiden, his initial encounter with a woman. The maiden appears to be an ideal for the youthful Parsifal. Was there a first love for you who inspired you as a young man?

Parsifal discovers that to become a knight he must be educated in the ways of knighthood. As a young man, what education did you receive or not receive concerning your manhood?

Parsifal makes an outrageous request that he be given the armor of the Red Knight. He is told he must earn it. As a young man, what outrageous demands might you have made of your parents, teachers or mentors?

What challenges did you have to accomplish to earn your name?

Who mentored you or taught you something valuable about being a man?

Part 3

Complete in his training, the young man set out on his journey. He met a maiden named Blanche Fleur, or White Flower. Her castle was under siege and she implored him: "Good Knight, I beg you to rescue my realm."

The young man, in single combat, conquered the commander and sent him to pledge fealty to the King. He returned to the castle of Blanche Fleur and spent a single night. Remembering the advice of his godfather, they slept together chaste in an intimate embrace: nose to nose, body to body, and toe to toe.

Leaving his true love, the young man traveled night and day until he came to a place where he found an old man was fishing. He asked the old man where he might stay for the night. The Fisher King invited the young man to his own home.

"Take this road a short way. You will find a drawbridge. Cross it."

Following these directions the young man found the Fisher King's castle and entered. The drawbridge immediately slammed close and locked.

The castle was magnificent. Four beautiful youths took his horse, bathed him, and offered him new clothing. They led him to a great hall filled with knights and their ladies, each bowing to him and greeting him as they met. It was a great feast, tables laden with fruits, vegetables and meats of all kinds.

At last, a great ceremony began, a procession that included three maidens who carried into the hall with great reverence: the Lance that pierced the side of the Christ as he was crucified on the Cross; the metal plate from which the Christ had eaten at the Last Supper; and, at last, the Grail, the brilliant cup the Christ drank from at the Last Supper.

The Fisher King was borne into the banquet on a splendid litter, moaning in agony. All the courtiers ate and drank from the Grail itself. Each was granted their heart's desire. A maiden brought forth a splendid sword which the Fisher King bestowed on the young man. It became the sword of his quest for all of his life.

Yet, he did not ask the question as commanded by Gournamond, his mentor, but followed his mother's advice to not ask too many questions, and he did not ask the crucial question: "Whom do you serve?"

Throughout the feast the Fisher King moaned and writhed in agony until four youths bore him from the great hall. The knights and ladies of the court dispersed. The youths led the young man to a bedchamber. In the morning the young man found himself alone in the forest. The castle was nowhere to be seen. The youth saddled his horse and rode on. On the way, he met a maiden crying. She explained that her knight had been killed. She asked the young man where he had been.

"I have been to a grand party in a magnificent hall at the center of a stalwart castle."

"That is impossible. This is a wasteland for miles around."

"I have seen maidens bearing a lance, a golden plate, and a great cup. I have seen a king borne in agony writhing on a litter."

"You have been to the Grail Castle," she responded. "What is your name?"

"Parsifal," erupted from the young man's lips.

Some questions you might ask yourself:

Parsifal is allowed to enter the Grail Castle. The hopes of the renewal of the kingdom rest on his young shoulders. Yet, he is still callow, obeying the advice of his mother rather than his mentor. Has there been a moment in your life when you might have stepped into your manhood but decided to remain in your youthful naiveté?

Parsifal finds himself outside of the Grail Castle, alone in the wasteland. The splendid castle has disappeared. Was there a time that you held a vision for your life but you were too young, inexperienced or unskilled to accomplish it? Did it seem to 'disappear' from your life and appear to be too overwhelming for you to accomplish?

Was there ever a time when you claimed your name, and proudly proclaimed who you are?

What might be a vision or quest that inspired you in your youth? Is there a vision you had as a youth that you have not completed? What quest might you now pursue in the second half of your life?

Part 4

Parsifal then began his long quest to protect the poor, right wrongs, slay dragons and save maidens. His fame grew from town to village to farm. His many deeds came to the ear of the King. The King left his court and vowed to find him.

Parsifal looked up one day and saw a single hawk about to drop down on three geese flying in the azure sky. Three drops of blood fell onto the pure white snow at his horse's hooves. He stopped, transfixed. An image of Blanche Fleur appeared and he stood entranced until the King's men found him and attempted to lead him to the King. Gently they took him to the King's court. The King embraced him and ordered three nights of feasting.

As the knights were cheering and eating and toasting, a hag riding a limping horse entered the court. From this mount, she recited and rebuked Parsifal for all his sins and said to all: "He failed to ask the question that would free us all, heal the land and restore justice!"

Parsifal left the feast humbled, silent and in despair. From the taunt of the hideous damsel he remembered his quest. He vowed to relentlessly search.

Twenty years passed. He grew bitterer, more forlorn, and more disillusioned. Many days he wandered aimlessly until he again remembered his quest.

At last he came to a group of pilgrims who had been traveling for many days. They said: "Why do you wear your armor on this day of days?"

"What day is this?"

"It is Good Friday, man! Come join us. We are traveling to the Forest Hermit. There you can confess and be shriven for Easter Sunday."

Parsifal stood before the hermit. The hermit berated him for his faults and failures and said: "But most of all, you have failed to ask the healing question in the Grail Castle!"

Then the hermit softened and said: "Go a little way. You will find a drawbridge. Cross the drawbridge into the castle."

Parsifal did, and again the drawbridge immediately drew up and again the door locked and again he entered the great hall, led by four beautiful youths. Here again was the great feast, and at the high point of the banquet, the maidens brought forth the Lance that pierced the side of the Christ, the golden plate and the Grail itself. The four youths bore the moaning Fisher King into the banquet hall.

Parsifal approached the agonizing King, and bent down to his ear and whispered: "Whom do you serve?"

A great wind blasted through the hall and all the doors opened at once. The King's skin grew white with radiance as he stood healed. The wasteland all around the great castle and throughout all the lands of the King immediately grew rich with bounty. Across the land there was the shouting of the people. It was the shouting of freedom.

Parsifal himself bowed down and knelt. The crown of the Grail King was bestowed upon him, and he became the King of Peace and Glory over all the land, bestowing wisdom to the youth, tending to the bounty, and bestowing great boons and blessings on his people.

Some questions you might ask yourself:

Parsifal spent many years as an active knight, doing knightly things. He created a legendary reputation that even inspired the King to bring him back to court. There the King created a three-day feast in his honor. Who in your life has honored you for your accomplishments? What of your life's work are you most proud?

Parsifal is allowed to enter the Grail Castle a second time, having confronted his shadows and fully lived the life of a warrior. What shadows might be preventing you from completing your warrior years and embracing the next stage of your life as a benevolent Vibrant Emeritus?

As he takes on the role of the Grail King, Parsifal steps into his Vibrant Emeritus life. What realms might you rule? How will you bestow blessings to these realms?

Elder Initiation: The Seven Tasks of the Vibrant Emeritus

Not all heroes' journeys end with transformation into vibrant eldering. The Parsifal legend takes us into the mystery of the last segment of life as a time of embracing abundance rather than lack, of measured justice and wisdom, and of blessing and giving. As with all stages of life, this important transition deserves a rite of passage into its singular mission that is rich with meaning and allows for the conscious embrace of the transformative tasks of men over 50.

Distilled from the work of many of the sources listed in the References section of this book are seven tasks suggested for fully living as a Vibrant Emeritus. As previously mentioned, these sources include the work of Allan Chinen, Angeles Arrien, John Robinson, Richard Rohr, Zalman Schachter-Shalomi and Michael Gurian. Each of the following chapters focuses on one of the seven tasks.

These are the Seven Tasks of the Vibrant Emeritus:

1. **Assessing the Journey So Far:** The Vibrant Emeritus is asked to look at one's heroic life so far, honor it, examine it for skills, knowledge and acumen that one might find useful in the next journey of life, and embrace a new purpose or mission. This accounting for one's life so far allows one to gauge one's skill, knowledge and successes as a platform for growth. As with all growth, the difficulty may be the letting go of the familiar and safe, of what has nourished one so far but may no longer be useful. Refusing to let go often means getting stuck.

2. **Confronting One's Shadows:** The Vibrant Emeritus confronts what Carl Jung called the Shadow: what we hide, repress and deny in our lives. Shadows often keep us from embracing personal growth. The Vibrant Emeritus discovers one's personal shadows in each of the four archetypes discussed by Robert Moore: King, Warrior, Magician and Lover. By confronting one's shadows and bringing them forward into the light, one can manage those forces that keep one from growing. Familiar shadows at this transitory stage of life might include: anger over the indignities of aging, despair over recuperating from losses, envy for what younger people still possess, and greed for more in life.

3. **Standing at the Crossroads:** The Vibrant Emeritus comes to a choice of continuing one's heroic adventuresome life while denying that one's energy will eventually flag, one's faculties will wane, and one might be overtaken by younger men and women. Or, one might embrace a new vision and mission for life even as one continues to pursue many of the activities one has formerly focused upon. The latter choice often leads to a life where one embraces one's mortality, deepens one's spirituality, and alters one's focus from oneself to others.

4. **Merging Innocence with Sagacity:** Having made the decision to move forward toward a new purpose in life while letting go of attachment to the heroic purposes of one's warrior years, the Vibrant Emeritus lays claim again to those youthful dreams and ideals, noble visions and higher callings that might have been daunting in one's youth but now seem achievable. This is the root of what Erik Erikson called "generativity". By combining the innocence of one's youthful intention with the skills,

knowledge, and experience of living, one finds one's personal wisdom. By merging innocence with sagacity, one affirms one's life and embraces one's most noble purpose with creativity and the courage to build one's legacy to enhance the lives of others, protect the planet, and move toward creating mankind's noblest aspirations.

5. **Deepening Spirituality:** This new life stance allows one to connect with one's deepest spirituality and life force. This is the deepening of connection to all that is around us, above us, below us and within us. In the words of the Navaho Indian Morning Greeting:

In beauty, may I walk. All the day long, may I walk.
Through the returning seasons, may I walk...
With beauty before me, may I walk...
With beauty behind me, may I walk...
With beauty above me, may I walk...
With beauty below me, may I walk...
With beauty all around me, may I walk...
In old age wandering on the trail of beauty, lively may I
    walk.
In old age wandering on a trail of beauty,
loving again, may I walk.
It is finished in beauty.
It is finished in beauty.

6. **Mentoring the Next Generation:** From all one has lived, learned, loved, and created, the Vibrant Emeritus now is able to mentor the next generation with wisdom, unconditional love, grace, and consistency. This mentoring connects the next generation with one's own and what has gone before. The Vibrant Emeritus prepares the next generation to take on the heroic challenges of their

Warrior years and to, in time, prepare for their own emeritus years.

7. **Embracing Death Consciously:** The Buddha gave up his corporeal manifestation, leaving his body and entering *parinirvana*. On the cross, Jesus commended his spirit unto his Father. Saint Francis embraced Sister Death. Mohammed chose union with God over this life when offered the choice. In each case the spiritual leader moved to a higher spiritual state consciously, achieving freedom, and initiating into a new consciousness. The final task is the ultimate letting go of all things from this life. It can be a time to fully embrace who one truly is.

The Vibrant Emeritus takes on these seven tasks, tasks that were taken by Elders generation after generation in traditional cultures. Elders can again earn the respect given formerly to them as they take on the tasks of renewing the earth, passing on wisdom, guiding and enlightening youth and preparing the culture to embrace its most noble purposes.

Chapter 2

Assessing the Journey So Far

I come to a place in the road. It is late and the weather is changing. I come to a place known as the Time of the Seven Tasks. I ask myself: Where have I been? What have I done? What have I learned? What have I collected? Do I need more? Who loves me? Whom do I love?
This is the first task.

All through our lives, we hoped to accomplish things. Now, hopefully, we can let our accomplishments shine with maturity and distinction in ways beyond desire and battle. "This is who I am," we say to the mirror. "This is what I represent; these are my accomplishments." If we say this at thirty, we're still not sure we're right. At seventy, we know we are. If we were people who hid our light previously, there is no reason to do so now.

And we have, hopefully by now, become Elders who understand what it means to say, as did the thirteenth-century Muslim poet Rumi: "The only way to measure myself is by the grandeur of what I love." We, our family, our community, and our legacy are the beloved. We are measured by them, do they know it? Now we can make sure everyone knows how important family is – family is one of the ways God makes the masterpiece of a life visible. Once we see this divinity clearly, we may feel a love for this beloved that drives us to give back, serve, and mentor family and friends (and the larger world) usefully and powerfully.

– Michael Gurian, *The Wonder of Aging*

The Task: Assessing the Journey So Far

The Vibrant Emeritus is asked to look at his heroic life so far, honor it, examine it for skills, knowledge and acumen that one might find useful in the next journey of life, and embrace a new purpose or mission. This accounting for one's life so far allows one to gauge one's skill, knowledge and successes as a platform for growth. As with all growth, the difficulty may be the letting go of the familiar and safe, of what has nourished one so far but may no longer be useful. Refusing to let go usually means getting stuck.

The first task for men consciously entering their eldering years is to take an assessment of the first half of one's life, celebrate one's accomplishments, honor one's disappointments and times of one's suffering, and then turn to the future and move on. Zalman Schachter-Shalomi and Ronald Miller in their profound book, *From Age-ing to Sage-ing*, speak of "harvesting". Harvesting allows one to examine both the triumphs and failures of one's life, celebrate the high points and low points as gifts that might empower and motivate later positive actions and in many cases provide knowledge and experience that ultimately enrich one's second half of life. They write:

> When we harvest, we consciously recognize and celebrate the contributions we have made in our career and family life. We also appreciate the friendships we have nurtured, the young people we have mentored and our wider involvements on behalf of the community, the nation and, ultimately, the Earth. Harvesting can be experienced from within as quiet self-appreciation or from without through the honor, respect, and recognition received from family members, relatives, colleagues at work and mentees...
>
> Harvesting shows us that we have made a difference in the world. We sense that our lives have meaning; that we have contributed to others, and that we are worthwhile human beings...
>
> We see that our rich fruit, and that even our failures,

stumblings and ill-conceived actions unwittingly have led to unexpected success and to a wisdom that is beyond any price tag.

Each of us comes to a time in our lives when we reach the gate of entering our Elder years. If we want we can stay standing there, aging. Aging is, of course, inevitable. Aging unconsciously usually leads to everything we fear about aging. Aging consciously allows us to embrace an entirely different point of view about our lives, our mission, and our future.

Like Parsifal, until this point most of us have been focused on challenge and achievement. For me, that meant learning more and more about presenting and facilitating skills. I found mentors, including NLP Master Michael Grinder, facilitation master Steve Zuieback, and youth development specialist Suze Rutherford. I expanded my expertise to include new strategies such as developing business leadership, fostering strategic planning, training presentation skills and leadership coaching. By the time I was fifty-five, I was considered a master trainer, facilitator, and coach in my field. I began to feel the call deep in my soul to give back. That is, to turn my consciousness toward developing a legacy.

I decided to write books that might help others who worked with youth. I decided to mentor others who wanted to learn presentation and facilitation skills. I decided to embrace my Elderhood. Younger men noticed and I was given a number of opportunities to mentor. I was asked by two ManKind Project leaders in the Kentucky region to take on the role of Ritual Elder at New Warrior Training Adventures. I began to look at how I might change my goals and direction toward letting go of ego, giving to others, and taking on new efforts to understand aging and Elders.

Over time, many men I have talked with about aging have discovered that what excited them most before age fifty concerned developing careers, owning property, building family and accumulating. After fifty, many men discover that these goals gradually lose meaning. Even greatly looked forward to experiences after retirement such as taking 'a trip of a lifetime' or what are often called 'leisure activities' lose their appeal. For a number of men, there comes a time when there is a deep yearning for something more in their lives. Some have noticed other aging men who seem to carry wisdom, who seem to attract younger men and women whom they then mentor, or who seem to be more at ease about the inevitable diminishment of physical and mental ability.

Parsifal entered this time when he meets the old man fishing, the Fisher King, for the second time. Men who fish together often reminisce. He is now ready to reenter the Grail Castle. He enters carrying within him the noble dreams and visions he had dreamed as a child, that were in his blood from his Warrior father. Having lived fully his Warrior life, he is able to transcend who he was and merge those youthful ideals with the practicality of knighthood and the wisdom gained from living. Within the Grail Castle, at the presentation of the lance and other relics of Christ's passion and death, he deepens his spirituality. His consciousness moves from the consciousness of the Warrior (egocentric, achievement-oriented and adventurous) to that of the Grail King: what Bill Plotkin calls "eco-centric" and "soul-centric," staying still, deeply spiritual, realm-ruling, blessing, giving and healing. With this new purpose, mission and vision, Parsifal heals the kingdom and the lands of his new realm flourished.

The Vibrant Emeritus, also, takes account of his life's adventures and achievements as he reenters his own Grail Castle, where once he had lived as the Golden Child in his childhood, and transcends his Warrior consciousness, merges his youthful ideals with his adult practicality and wisdom, and claims his kingdom not as a King.

Like it or not, aging means letting go until we ultimately let go of life when we die. We can choose to let this happen, slouching toward death in fear and self-loathing, in disappointment and trying to hang on to what we once might have been. Or, we can choose to assess and celebrate what we have accomplished and honor our achievements. And then let them go.

The great challenge of Task One is to let go. Our lives have been ego-driven, self-centered, and achievement-oriented. Letting go of the ego focus that we have lived for most of our lives, that has stoked and stroked us, and that we often have made the definition of who we are as men seems counterintuitive. Because we live at a time and in a culture where Elders are dismissed, when youth is honored, when huge amounts of money are spent on looking younger, taking on youthful challenges, and piling up the desires of youth (younger partners, cooler cars, vacation homes) it takes a courageous and deeply masculine man to take another path. My belief is that not accepting ourselves as Elders means that we turn our back on a natural human process.

How we live as the industrial age gives way to an information, data-driven, technological age is not how men lived and perceived themselves for millennia. It is only since the Industrial Revolution that aging men have been cast aside. Men who had worked in factories no longer had skills and techniques related to work that they could pass on to the next generation as they had as farmers and earlier as hunters. Gradually, Elders lost their position as community leaders while youthful vitality replaced Elder sagacity. As the culture moved to honoring youth, Elders became only a reminder of the diminishment age brings. For thousands of years, humans understood all of the stages of life from conception to death because these life dramas played out within the intergenerational home itself – the cabin, the lodge, the dwelling within the village. Now these natural processes take place out of sight. We have chosen not to witness childbirth, disease, late-stage aging, and death if possible, making these the province of hospitals and nursing homes.

At the Elder's Gate, we are challenged to return to our deep humanity as men, to the natural rhythms of life: a life that brings us to an honorable and esteemed period of blessing, wisdom and mentoring after the adventure of our Warrior years. It means embracing a new vibrancy, new self-definition, and a new personal mission.

This challenge is not easy. How many aging men in our lives are stymied by this decision? How many men continue to attempt to do what they always have done, even in the face of younger men challenging their positions; the aging of body, mind and spirit; and the negative vision the present culture holds onto regarding aging? How many men in their fifties and sixties approach their later years paralyzed by fear? Or, by buying into the new industry of hair dyes, Botox, exercise equipment, and the empty promises of never having to age? How many men say, "I'm not ready yet, I'm not ready for the Way of the Old Geezer?"

So, standing at the Elder's Gate, the task is to assess. Honestly. Fearlessly. Humbly. Resolutely.

The first step of the task is to listen deeply to the stirrings within that begin to call to one. Like a day late in summer when one feels a slight chill and suddenly one recognizes that summer is ending and soon the leaves will turn. It might be an impulse to stop momentarily and to look back at one's life. It might be a thought that one might want to look at the legacy of one's life, what one might pass on to one's children, to those following one in the work that one does, or to the community that has sustained one.

Assessment means not only looking at honoring and celebrating. It is also examining what one defines as one's failures, times one might wish one had a 'do over,' disappoint-ments, and unfulfilled desires. It means letting go of the impact of ancient wounds, of self-deprecating beliefs about oneself, and the 'what-might-have-beens.' Perhaps even more difficult, the task often involves letting go of seeking achievements, personal acquirement, and ego-driven activities. This might mean letting go of how we have been raised to be men. Most of the role models and cultural heroes, especially in the post-industrial/ information age, are those who have made it 'big time.' So much so, that many of the heroes in the Western world presently are multimillionaire athletes (surely, the highest form of youth-worship).

At the very same time, what makes the decision to move from Warrior to Elder difficult is the scarcity of positive Elder role models. Elders we might admire such as Gandhi, Martin Luther King, Nelson Mandela, and Jimmy Carter are either dead or dying. Living Elder statesmen like Bill Clinton are often discussed concerning their flaws. Are they our wounded Fisher Kings?

If we, as men, are to transcend ourselves as Warriors and become generative, inspiring and giving as Elders, we must meet Task One.

A Classic Tale

The Water of Life
(Grimm's Fairy Tales)
Long before you or I were born, there reigned, in a country a great way off, a king who had three sons. This king fell very ill. He was so ill that nobody thought he could live. His sons were very much grieved at their father's sickness; and as they were walking together very mournfully in the garden of the palace, a little old man met them and asked, "What is the matter?"

They told him that their father was very ill, and that they were afraid nothing could save him.

"I know what would," said the little old man, "it is the Water of Life. If he could have a draught of it he would be well again; but it is very hard to get."

Then the eldest son said, "I will soon find it;" and he went to the sick king, and begged that he might go in search of the Water of Life, as it was the only thing that could save him.

"No," said the king. "I had rather die than place you in such great danger as you must meet with in your journey."

But he begged so hard that the king let him go; and the prince thought to himself, "If I bring my father this water, he will make me sole heir to his kingdom."

Then he set out and when he had gone on his way some time he came to a deep valley, overhung with rocks and woods; and as he looked around, he saw standing above him on one of the rocks a little ugly dwarf, with a sugarloaf cap and a scarlet cloak.

The dwarf called to him and said, "Prince, whither so fast?"

"What is that to thee, you ugly imp?" said the prince haughtily and rode on.

But the dwarf was enraged at his arrogance and laid a fairy spell of ill-luck upon him; so that as he rode on the mountain pass became narrower and narrower, and at last the way was so straitened that he could not go to step forward: and when he thought to have turned his horse round and go back the way he came, he heard a loud laugh ringing round him, and found that the path was closed behind him, so that he was shut in all round. He next tried to get off his horse and make his way on foot, but again the laugh rang in his ears, and he found himself unable to move a step, and thus he was forced to abide spellbound.

Meantime, the old king was lingering on in daily hope of his son's return, till at last the second son said, "Father, I will go in search of the Water of Life," for he thought to himself, "My brother is surely dead, and the kingdom will fall to me if I find the water."

The king was at first very unwilling to let him go, but at last yielded to his wish. So he set out and followed the same road which his brother had done, and met with the same dwarf who had stopped him at the same spot in the mountains, saying, as before, "Prince, prince, whither so fast?"

"Mind your own affairs, busybody!" said the prince scornfully and rode on.

But the dwarf put the same spell upon him as he put on his elder brother, and he, too, was at last obliged to take up his abode in the heart of the mountains. Thus it is with proud silly people, who think themselves above everyone else, and are too proud to ask or take advice.

When the second prince had thus been gone a long time, the youngest son said he would go and search for the Water of Life, and trusted he should soon be able to make his father well again. So he set out, and the dwarf met him too at the same spot in the valley, among the mountains, and said, "Prince, whither so fast?"

And the prince said, "I am going in search of the Water of Life, because my father is ill and like to die: Can you help me? Pray be kind, and aid me if you can!"

"Do you know where it is to be found?" asked the dwarf.

"No," said the prince, "I do not. Pray tell me if you know."

"Then as you have spoken to me kindly, and are wise enough to seek for advice, I will tell you how and where to go. The water you seek springs from a well in an enchanted castle. That you may be able to reach it in safety, I will give you an iron wand and two little loaves of bread. Strike the iron door of the castle three times with the wand, and it will open: Two hungry lions will be lying down inside gaping for their prey, but if you throw them the bread they will let you pass. Then hasten on to the well, and take some of the Water of Life before the clock strikes twelve; for if you tarry longer the door will shut upon you forever."

Then the prince thanked his little friend with the scarlet cloak for his friendly aid, and took the wand and the bread, and went traveling on and on, over sea and over land, till he came to his journey's end, and found everything to be as the dwarf had told him. The door flew open at the third stroke of the wand, and when the lions were quieted he went on through the castle and came at length to a beautiful hall. Around it he saw several knights sitting in a trance. He pulled off their rings and put them on his own fingers. In another room he saw on a table a sword and a loaf of bread, which he also took. Further on he came to a room where a beautiful young lady sat upon a couch; and she welcomed him joyfully. She said, if he would set her free from the spell that bound her, the kingdom should be his, if he would come back in a year and marry her. Then she told him that the well that held the Water of Life was in the palace gardens; and bade him make haste, and draw what he wanted before the clock struck twelve.

He walked on; and as he walked through beautiful gardens he came to a delightful shady spot in which stood a couch. He thought to himself, as he felt tired, that he would rest himself for a while, and gaze on the lovely scenes around him. So he laid himself down and sleep fell upon him unawares, so that he did not wake up till the clock was striking a quarter to twelve. Then he sprang from the couch dreadfully frightened, ran to the well, filled a cup that was standing by him full of water, and hastened to get away in time. Just as he was going out of the iron door it struck twelve, and the door fell so quickly upon him that it snapped off a piece of his heel.

When he found himself safe, he was overjoyed to think that he had got the Water of Life; and as he was going on his way homewards, he passed by the little dwarf, who, when he saw the sword and the loaf, said, "You have made a noble prize." With the sword you can at a blow slay whole armies, and the bread will never fail you."

Then the prince thought to himself, "I cannot go home to my father without my brothers;" so he said, "My dear friend, cannot you tell me where my two brothers are, who set out in search of the Water of Life before me, and never came back?"

"I have shut them up by a charm between two mountains,"

said the dwarf, "because they were proud and ill-behaved, and scorned to ask advice."

The prince begged so hard for his brothers that the dwarf at last set them free, though unwillingly, saying, "Beware of them, for they have bad hearts."

Their brother, however, was greatly rejoiced to see them, and told them all that had happened to him: how he had found the Water of Life, and had taken a cup full of it; and how he had set a beautiful princess free from a spell that bound her; and how she had engaged to wait a whole year, and then to marry him and to give him the kingdom.

Then they all three rode on together. On their way home they came to a country that was laid waste by war and a dreadful famine, so that it was feared all must die for want. But the prince gave the king of the land the bread, and all his kingdom ate of it. And he lent the king the wonderful sword, and he slew the enemy's army with it; and thus the kingdom was once more in peace and plenty. In the same manner he befriended two other countries through which they passed on their way.

When they came to the sea, they got onto a ship and during their voyage the two eldest said to themselves, "Our brother has got the water which we could not find, therefore our father will forsake us and give him the kingdom, which is our right." So they were full of envy and revenge, and agreed together how they could ruin him. Then they waited till he was fast asleep, and poured the Water of Life out of the cup, and took it for themselves, giving him bitter seawater instead.

When they came to their journey's end, the youngest son brought his cup to the sick king, that he might drink and be healed. Scarcely, however, had he tasted the bitter seawater when he became worse even than he was before. Then both the elder sons came in and blamed the youngest for what they had done. They said that he wanted to poison their father, but that they had found the Water of Life, and had brought it with them. He no sooner began to drink of what they brought him, then he felt his sickness leave him and he was as strong and well as in his younger days.

Then they went to their brother and laughed at him saying, "Well, brother, you found the Water of Life, did you? You have had the trouble and we shall have the reward. Pray, with all your cleverness, why did not you manage to keep your eyes open? Next year one of us will take away your beautiful princess, if you do not take care. You had better say nothing about this to our father, for he does not believe a word you say. If you tell tales, you shall lose your life in the bargain: but be quiet, and we will let you off."

The old king was still very angry with his youngest son, and thought that he really meant to have taken away his life; so he called his court together, and asked what should be done, and all agreed that he ought to be put to death. The prince knew nothing of what was going on till one day when the king's chief huntsman went a-hunting with him. They were alone in the wood together. The huntsman looked so sorrowful that the prince said, "My friend, what is the matter with you?"

"I cannot and dare not tell you," said he.

But the prince begged very hard, and said, "Only tell me what it is, and do not think I shall be angry, for I will forgive you."

"Alas!" said the huntsman. "The king has ordered me to shoot you."

The prince started at this, and said, "Let me live, and I will change dresses with you. You shall take my royal coat to show to my father, and do you give me your shabby one."

"With all my heart," said the huntsman. "I am sure I shall be glad to save you, for I could not have shot you." Then he took the prince's coat, and gave him the shabby one, and went away through the wood.

Sometime after, three grand embassies came to the old king's court with rich gifts of gold and precious stones for his youngest son. Now, all these were sent from the three kings to whom he had lent his sword and loaf of bread, in order to rid them of their enemy and feed their people. This touched the old king's heart, and he thought his son might still be guiltless, and said to his court, "O that my son were still alive! How it grieves me that I had him killed!"

"He is still alive," said the huntsman, "and I am glad that I had pity on him, but let him go in peace, and brought home his royal coat."

At this the king was overwhelmed with joy, and made it known throughout all his kingdom that if his son would come back to his court he would forgive him.

Meanwhile, the princess was eagerly waiting till her deliverer should come back; and had a road made leading up to her palace all of shining gold. She told her courtiers that whoever came on horseback, and rode straight up to the gate upon it, was her true Lover; and that they must let him in: but whoever rode on one side of it, they must be sure was not the right one; and that they must send him away at once.

The time soon came when the eldest brother thought that he would make haste to go to the princess and say that he was the one who had set her free, and that he should have her for his wife, and the kingdom with her. As he came before the palace and saw the golden road, he stopped to look at it, and he thought to himself, "It is a pity to ride upon this beautiful road;" so he turned aside and rode on the right-hand side of it. But when he came to the gate, the guards, who had seen the road he took, said to him that he could not be what he said he was, and must go about his business.

The second prince set out soon afterwards on the same errand; and when he came to the golden road, and his horse had set one foot upon it, he stopped to look at it, and thought it very beautiful. He said to himself, "What a pity it is that anything should tread here!" Then he too turned aside and rode on the left side of it. But when he came to the gate the guards said he was not the true prince, and that he too must go away about his business; and away he went.

Now when the full year was come round, the third brother left the forest in which he had lain hid for fear of his father's anger, and set out in search of his betrothed bride. So he journeyed on, thinking of her all the way, and rode so quickly that he did not even see what the road was made of, but went with his horse straight over it; and as he came to the gate it flew open. The princess welcomed him with joy, and said he was her deliverer, and should now be her husband and lord of the kingdom. When the first joy at their meeting was over, the princess told him she had heard of his father having forgiven him, and of his wish to have him home again. So, before his wedding with the princess, he went to visit his father, taking her with him. Then he told him everything; how his brothers had cheated and robbed him, and yet that he had borne all those wrongs for the love of his father. And the old king was very angry, and wanted to punish his wicked sons; but they made their escape, and got onto a ship and sailed away over the wide sea. Where they went to nobody knew and nobody cared.

And now the old king gathered together his court, and asked all his kingdom to come and celebrate the wedding of his son and the princess. And young and old, noble and squire, gentle and simple, came at once on the summons; and among the rest came the friendly dwarf, with the sugarloaf hat, and a new scarlet cloak.

And the wedding was held, and the merry bells rung.

And all the good people they danced and they sung,

And feasted and frolick'd I can't tell how long.

Some Questions to Reflect Upon:

As with looking at dreams where all the characters often represent an aspect of one's inner life, the characters in the classic tales often represent different archetypes within the persona. In this story the king is ill, similar to the wounded grail king in the Parsifal story. When the king is not healthy, the kingdom suffers, becomes a wasteland, and everyone is at stasis, unable to move toward health, healing and growth. Where in your life might you be stuck, denying yourself personal growth?

The Water of Life is needed to replenish and nourish the king and the kingdom. The elder brothers go on a quest to find the water, but ignore the dwarf and follow the traditional search which leads them both to getting stuck, as the king is stuck. Their inability to accept advice or new ideas, their following of what has always been true, condemns them to narrow vision. Where might you be unable to let go, consider new options and revive your life?

It is the youngest brother who is flexible, accepts perspective from an unlikely source and who perseveres and finds the Water of Life. How might you expand your vision, become mentally and spiritually flexible, and become generative of healing?

The older brothers are duplicitous and jaded. Like Parsifal, who enters his life as a knight from a place of innocence, the youngest brother seeks for the Water of Life without pre-conceptions. How might you delve into your childhood innocence to revive your life as you enter into your Elder days?

A Contemporary Story: My Uncle

I have a great uncle. He is great in many ways. He was a fighter pilot in the Korean Conflict. When he mustered out, he used the GI Bill to get his college degree. In our culture, the military, the university and first work provide the most cogent of initiatory experiences into young adult life – though they are not consciously or ritually designed to do so. Young men are left mostly on their own. Sometimes they find a mentor, if they are fortunate and are open to a mentoring relationship.

As a fighter pilot, my uncle became a Warrior. He flew life and death missions. He was only 18. He entered his Warrior years with a clear demarcation between his youth on a farm near the Ohio River and fighting with other young men in a war.

When he returned, he used the GI Bill to finance a degree in business. And he got a job in an industry he would work in for the next forty years of his life. This second initiation into his work life altered his Warrior status from war to peace in the early 1950s. Still the Warrior/hero patterns he had learned in the military served him well. He was ready to hook his dreams to the star of success that American business provided in the corporate world. He was unafraid to move his young wife and family as the challenges of the corporate ladder moved them around the country. He was unafraid to take on new work and larger territories as the company expanded. He learned the culture of the corporation and how to be successful, in the office and at the country club.

After many moves, larger and more expensive houses in plumb locations near both oceans, and as a vice president, he was ready for the final challenge, the ultimate success story when the bottom fell out. The company decided to look outside the corporation for its next leader. My uncle was given a golden parachute. For twelve months he took his company car to his office every workday and read the *Wall Street Journal* while his Executive Assistant filed and repainted her nails. Every day, until he was given a hollow retirement party at age 54.

And then my uncle, for the first time in his life, was stuck.

He did some consulting work at whatever fee he set and he set astronomical fees, until he got bored. He played golf when invited but never joined a club. He looked for property and a community to settle in, in the Northwest, Midwest and South. He ended up living in his wife's father's house. Slowly, as his retirement grew into his seventies and eighties, he more and more lived in the past and reminisced about what might have been.

His children moved to places far away from their parents. And then my aunt died and my uncle stayed in his father-in-law's house and infrequently visited his children for short visits, not exactly estranged but not building enriching and loving relationships in the present either. And he has had no thoughts of mentoring and empowering his own grandchildren. When asked about it, his answer was simple: "People fall into two categories: Givers and Takers. I'm a Taker."

As I enter my own years after career, my children grown and making families of their own, I ask myself, am I a Giver or a Taker? And the answer is both. Wisdom literature tells us that to give to others is, in fact, giving to oneself. But there is also the part of me that, if I am not aware of my shadows, manipulates and takes even in the guise of giving. I look at the restlessness of my uncle and his gift to me is a lesson in what happens when even a highly aware and intelligent man finds himself unable to move on through the gates that lead to becoming a Vibrant Emeritus. I see what happens when one gets stuck on the journey.

I ask myself, am I stuck like the egocentric, narrow-minded princes who are unable to heal the king and turn the wasteland into a garden; or am I flexible, creative and resourceful like the third son, who heals and transforms?

Discussion

The beginning of an initiation into transcendent Eldering often begins with taking stock of one's life, assessing what one might want to take into the next phase and what to leave behind (including the 'laurels' of accomplishment, disappointments and fear, and attachment to both what was and what might have been). By taking on this challenge, one can build a platform for personal growth and the reclamation of the vibrancy and vitality of ideals, values, dreams and aspirations that might have been daunting at the beginning of one's adult life – or pushed aside in order take care of business and family and to establish one's life. This is a good time for one who is entering the second half of life to take a good look at where one has been.

The uncle in the story is quite willing to look back over his life, especially as it triggers a desire to find something lost there. The trap he has fallen into, starting at the age of 54, is getting stuck there, unable to get unstuck and to move forward. He, unfortunately, blocks any thought of letting go of the past, of his money, of his memories, of what might have been so that he might have a new vision for his future. He prefers the 'comfort' of staying put, but denies himself a rich and vibrant life for himself in the present.

The challenge of aging that he failed to meet was the task of examining one's life as one moves away from one's working years, and honoring and celebrating his skills, experiences and achievements and moving forward into the last stage of his life. So there he was, with many times over a million dollars in his bank and investments; with skills, insights and experiences that might have been used to foster growth in himself, his children and grandchildren and in the community; without positive direction into the future. He appeared to be thwarted from growing into Erik Erikson's "generativity" that might have saved his Elder soul. Rather, he preferred the ghosts and shadows of the past and what might have been.

Unlike the process of entering into adulthood my uncle experienced through war, university, and work, there were (and are) few societal and recognizable rites of initiation into being an Elder. Thus, men who simply grow old are not necessarily recognized as Elders. In a culture more and more desirous of youth and a youth culture, Elders are no longer recognized as a revered and noble group, honored by the population and listened to for their guidance and wisdom. Where older men once mentored men into the skills they had taken a lifetime to learn, such as farming, the making of valued objects, dignity, integrity and responsibility, we see a culture desperate for those skills and values.

From a life assessment, one can build a legacy beyond the accumulation of objects and money. One can reclaim one's soul. Here, below, are a series of challenges designed to help one accomplish the first task of the Vibrant Emeritus.

Challenges

Challenge One: Writing Your Story

1. Reflect on the classic tale of *The Water of Life* and think about its themes, its use of archetypes, and its perspectives on growth, change, and healing.
2. Reflect on the contemporary story and how it connects with the classic tale.
3. Reflect on your own journey so far, and write your own contemporary story and where you see yourself right now in your life.

Challenge Two: Life Journey Visualization

1. Either read the following visualization into a recorder so that you can play it to yourself or ask a person you trust to read it to you. Make sure to pause for five to ten seconds at the end of each line.
2. Place a notebook or journal next to you with your favorite pen.
3. Playing soft, meditative music can enhance the experience.
4. Follow the direction of the visualization narrative:

I invite you to lie down on your back in a place where you feel alone,
Just relax and breathe deeply
A deep cleansing breath
Take a deep breath through your nose and hold it

And let it go slowly out your mouth
(do this 3 more times)
And now as you relax and breathe normally concentrate on
the breath as it enters and leaves your nostrils
Just at the place where the breath comes and goes
Until you are completely relaxed
Your neck and shoulders are relaxed
Let go of any tension there
Let go
Of any tension in your core, your belly and lower back, just
relax
Let go
Of any tension in your hips, your thighs, just relax
Let go
Of any tension in your calves, your knees
Let go
Of any tension in your ankles and feet
Just relax and concentrate on your breath
Coming and going, coming and going
And as you relax imagine that you are out for a walk
It's a fine fall day and you feel fine
The leaves are changing, the wind carries a chill
Still it is warm, the sun shining through the trees
The leaves fall slowly, one by one
You come to an unfamiliar part of the woods
A path not as yet taken by you
The leaves are crunchy under your feet
They make a crumbling sound as you walk
The path leads into a thicket,
There are brilliant splashes of light ahead
As the path turns, you come to a gate
It is a large gate, like the gate to an estate
The gate is formidable and you wonder if you can open it
You wonder if you should open it.

Looking around, you see a great log at the side of the path
The huge log sits next to an oak tree
You can sit on the log and rest your back
You sit and stretch your legs and find your comfort against
the tree
Looking up, you see fluffy clouds making shapes against the
azure sky
Your mind wanders back, back
Back to a time when you were young
Maybe just a boy with a casual walking stick
Maybe your first walk alone in the woods
On another great fall day
You remember breathing the chill air deep into your lungs
As you do now, breathe in deep the autumn air
As you breathe and sit your mind goes further back
Back to your early memories
Back, back to your earliest memory
Back to the one memory you can still remember as the earliest
memory
And sitting there now with your earliest memory
You begin to remember again how fine it was to be young
Maybe you remember a prize you won
Or the day you finally accomplished a challenge
A challenge you had wanted to accomplish for awhile
Something that made you proud
Something others noticed you doing
You might have learned that you liked accomplishing things
You might have begun to set yourself challenges
Maybe at sports, maybe at school, maybe with your friends,
You might have had long thoughts, deep dreams
So you might have tested yourself against other boys
Then, later against other young men
Maybe you started to set goals for yourself as a man
Maybe you found conquests that motivated you

Told you that you were better than others
Maybe you found you liked to collect things
An apartment or a house, a car
A bigger house, a cooler car
Maybe you judged yourself against others as to what you had
The experiences you had, the places you traveled to
The women or men you conquered
Maybe you strove to make more money
Maybe you strove to get a better work position
Or maybe you strove to build your own work
Maybe you took pride in your family, your children
And maybe you set goals and achievements for your children
And when they scored, won, achieved you felt proud
Maybe there were hard times growing up
Times you might not want to remember
But remembering them you find a gift
An unexpected gift that helped you grow
That helped you become the man you are today
Maybe there are memories you'd rather forget
But you can't, you still hold on to them
Now maybe your family has grown and left home
Maybe work isn't as challenging as it once was
Maybe taking another trip isn't as exciting
Maybe what you thought would be a great lifestyle after
    working isn't
Maybe you wonder, is that all there is?
Maybe you look longingly through the gate to see if there is
    something new
Looking through the gate you notice someone coming toward
    you on the other side
It is an Elder, a man you admire
A man you'd like to become
But you're not sure how
Maybe the Elder is someone you've noticed or met

Maybe the Elder is someone you know about
Maybe the Elder reminds you of yourself in some way
But maybe you think, "Not yet" or "I'm not ready."
Looking at the gate you notice it is made up of reasons not to
　　go through
So you lay back and take account of who you are
And you put aside times you'd like to forget
And you focus on your achievement, where you have come to
It feels good on the sunny log, taking stock
So you lie back against the tree trunk
And you celebrate what has passed and where you are
And leaning back you breathe deeply
Gradually you come back into the room
The tree becomes the floor
Slowly, gradually you open your eyes
When you are ready you look around,
But before you get up, you pick up your favorite pen
In your notebook or journal you take stock of your life
List your memories, even the sad ones and ones you'd like to
　　forget;
When you have listed as many memories you can list, write
　　about the Elder you saw
Making sure to describe his appearance, energy, desires,
　　hopes and dreams.

Challenge Three: Life Journey Map

Carl Jung has suggested that one's challenge for the first half of
life is to build a strong ego, and the task of the second half of life
is letting it go to enter a time of deeper connection to one's self
and to others.

Ego serves one well whose challenge is to compete for status
and power, to collect objects and fortune, and to provide one's
family with larger and more expensive property. Ego does little
for men (and women) who come to the crossroads of life, feeling

empty and questioning life's purpose, no longer focused (from choice or having been pushed out in some way) on the status of ego, who want to find new purpose.

Ultimately, as one's life comes to completion, one faces the challenge of renunciation of all but one's soul.

The challenge suggested here is to map one's life so far, use it as a gloss to examine and assess where one finds oneself as one enters what Michael Gurian calls the Transitional Stage of becoming an Elder (embracing one's Elder years consciously and with purpose rather than simply aging aimlessly). It works well to do this challenge with either a trusted partner (who also takes on this challenge) or with a small group.

Instructions:

1. Take a large sheet of drawing paper and with a thin marker indicate areas of your life. You might start at the top left-hand portion of the paper and label it "Where I Come From." Using notations you might consider several meanings for "Where I Come From." Here are some possible meanings:
   One's personal heritage: one's genealogical stock
   One's geographical heritage: what part of the country, culture
   One's parentage, one's family of origin
   One's family values
   One's personal philosophy – such as "where I'm coming from"

2. Draw a line and indicate a second area labeled "Times I'd Do Over." This area might contain notes on areas of one's life one might do over because one felt particular joy and pleasure or times one might want a 'do over' in order to reclaim, from failure, an embarrassment or a time one would rather forget.

3. Draw a line and indicate a new area where your life line

goes up and down to show "Ups and Downs" in my life. Include the highest highs and deepest downs.

4. Include three fundamental things you believe from the first half of your life.

5. Finally, indicate a final area: "Where I Seem to be Heading." List several directions you might take next.

6. When finished, show your partner or the group your map. Let them examine your map for about a minute or two before you tell your life story using the map.

7. When you finish your story, ask your partner or group to do the following: Ask questions for clarity only. Ask them to tell you how they felt when they heard a part of the story that resonated for them.

Challenge Four: Personal Eulogy

The classic movie, *Citizen Kane*, begins with a newsreel of the life of the fictional 'great man' Charles Foster Kane. Unsatisfied with the newsreel as it stands as a monument to Kane's life, the producers send reporters out to find out the meaning of Kane's dying word, "Rosebud," to see if it gives a clue to the meaning of his life. As famous men age, newspapers, magazines and news departments at television stations keep files and create eulogies prior to these famous men's deaths so that they can quickly produce a life story.

The challenge here is to review one's Life Journey Map completed in the challenge above and to celebrate the accomplishments, struggles, sufferings, triumphs and meaning of one's life so far.

Write your own eulogy containing the suggested elements. When finished, find a trusted friend to whom you want to read it. Or, using the Life Journey Map as a template, talk out your eulogy for your friend. Then, ask the listener if he or she believes it is accurate, and together see if you can discover the themes and meanings of your life so far.

Challenge Five: Funeral Pyre

In several cultures, when a hero died he was given a "Hero's Funeral" on a funeral pyre. In this case, we want to honor and remember our heroic adventures but let them go as we embrace a new consciousness and transcend to the Vibrant Emeritus status of abundant living, blessing and mentoring. The focus shifts from one's accomplishments to supporting and empowering younger men and women.

The challenge is to let go of one's life so far so that one can focus on becoming one's generative self and one can look forward to future accomplishments as a mentoring Elder: one who blesses, reconciles, honors heroes on their heroic journey, speaks from wisdom and integrates the visions and ideals of one's youth.

Taking the Life Journey Map constructed above, turn it over and tear out or cut out small pieces of paper large enough to write a few words (no more than a sentence) or draw symbols that indicate the following:

A hope you have for your life
A resentment you need to let go of
A person you need to forgive
A forgiveness you hope to receive
A forgiveness you need to give
A personal loss
A sadness
A victory or triumph
A personal passion
A place you hope to see
Something you hope to accomplish
An experience that gives you strength
A time of personal suffering
A turn in the road
An unexpected boon

A wrench thrown in
A skill you intend to use
An understanding that keeps you balanced
A dream you hold onto

If possible, ask the person you worked with on the Personal Eulogy to witness as you read each item or show the symbol you made, fold up, and piece by piece throw into a fire. Use either a setting with a fireplace or use an outdoor caldron. Take a deep breath as you toss in each piece.

A Poem to Contemplate

Ulysses
By Alfred, Lord Tennyson

It little profits that an idle king,
By this still hearth, among these barren crags,
Matched with an aged wife, I mete and dole
Unequal laws unto a savage race,
That hoard, and sleep, and feed, and know not me.

I cannot rest from travel: I will drink
Life to the lees: all times I have enjoyed
Greatly, have suffered greatly, both with those
That loved me, and alone; on shore, and when
Through scudding drifts the rainy Hyades
Vext the dim sea: I am become a name;
For always roaming with a hungry heart
Much have I seen and known; cities of men
And manners, climates, councils, governments,
Myself not least, but honoured of them all;
And drunk delight of battle with my peers;
Far on the ringing plains of windy Troy.

I am part of all that I have met;
Yet all experience is an arch where through
Gleams that blessed world, whose margin fades
For ever and for ever when I move.
How dull it is to pause, to make an end,
To rust unburnished, not to shine in use!
As though to breathe were life. Life piled on life
Were all too little, and of one to me
Little remains: but every hour is saved
From that eternal silence, something more,
A bringer of new things; and vile it were
For some three suns to store and hoard myself,
And this gray spirit yearning in desire
To follow knowledge like a sinking star,
Beyond the utmost bound of human thought.

This is my son, mine own Telemachus,
To whom I leave the sceptre and the isle
Well-loved of me, discerning to fulfill
This labour, by slow prudence to make mild
A rugged people, and through soft degrees
Subdue them to the useful and the good.
Most blameless is he, centred in the sphere
Of common duties, decent not to fail
In offices of tenderness, and pay
Meet adoration to my household gods,
When I am gone. He works his work, I mine.

There lies the port; the vessel puffs her sail:
There gloom the dark broad seas. My mariners,
Souls that have toiled, and wrought, and thought with me
That ever with a frolic welcome took
The thunder and the sunshine, and opposed
Free hearts, free foreheads you and I are old;

Old age had yet his honour and his toil;
Death closes all: but something ere the end,
Some work of noble note, may yet be done,
Not unbecoming men that strove with Gods.
The lights begin to twinkle from the rocks:
The long day wanes: the slow moon climbs: the deep
Moans round with many voices. Come, my friends,
'Tis not too late to seek a newer world.
Push off, and sitting well in order smite
The sounding furrows; for my purpose holds
To sail beyond the sunset, and the baths
Of all the western stars, until I die.
It may be that the gulfs will wash us down:
It may be we shall touch the Happy Isles,
And see the great Achilles, whom we knew.
Though much is taken, much abides; and though
We are not now that strength which in the old days
Moved earth and heaven; that which we are, we are,
One equal-temper of heroic hearts,
Made weak by time and fate, but strong in will
To strive, to seek, to find, and not to yield.

Some Questions to Reflect Upon:

The Odyssey ends with Odysseus (Ulysses) overcoming the legions of suitors who are waiting to claim his wife, Penelope; exile his son; and conquer his kingdom. Reinstalled as king, the story ends with the hero and his wife sitting across from one another in silence. The hero has come home. Quite frequently this is the end of hero tales. But Alfred, Lord Tennyson, in his poem Ulysses *imagines a restless king who longs for a return to adventure. Is this Ulysses embracing his Vibrant Emeritus status, or is he simply stuck, unable to transcend this position and let go of his heroic past?*

How might you characterize Ulysses? Happy? Trapped in his heroic life? Sad, yet yearning for his former life? Heroically discontent?

Is Ulysses moving into a time of spiritual Eldering and vibrancy? Or is he simply off again, unable to move into a new vision and direction for his life?

Practice

Gratitude Journal

One may want to continue to celebrate the past and perhaps look at some events, as they come up in your memory, to reframe events that might be regretful or seen as an obstacle to fully embracing the future. The suggestion is to keep a "Gratitude Journal" where you note these events. One way to keep this journal includes these steps:

1. Write down the event as objectively as possible.
2. Reflect on the event, writing down any feelings you might be feeling from reviewing this event.
3. If the event is one you might want to reframe, that is, look at differently and in the context of your entire life so far, attempt to see this event as one that taught you something you needed to know, showed you that you might want to make other choices, or how the event turned out to be unwittingly a positive experience.

Growth Questions

Discuss the following questions with a friend or consider what they evoke in you in a journal:

Of which of my accomplishments am I most proud?

What time of suffering do I believe changed me the most?

Did suffering lead to new vision, new opportunity, or new realizations?

Based on my life so far, what knowledge, understandings, or wisdom would I share with a young person?

What is most difficult for me to complete this task, the task of letting go and moving on to a new way of addressing life in my Elder years?

Did I have any older role models who influenced me for better or worse?

What word or phrase might sum up my adventurous and heroic life so far?

Chapter 3

Confronting Shadows

I come to a place in the road where the shadows are long and dark. I ask myself: What is the mask I wear? As a Lover? As a Warrior? As a Magician? As a King? What masks must I shed?
This is the second task.

Unfortunately there can be no doubt that man is, on the whole, less good than he imagines himself or wants to be. Everyone carries a shadow, and the less it is embodied in the individual's conscious life, the blacker and denser it is. If an inferiority is conscious, one always has a chance to correct it. Furthermore, it is constantly in contact with other interests, so that it is continually subjected to modifications. But if it is repressed and isolated from consciousness, it never gets corrected.

– Carl Jung, *Psychology and Religion*

The Task: Confronting Shadows

The second task is to examine the shadows that often drive our behavior and create the masks we wear in the belief that we can hide, repress and deny our true selves. The task here is for us to embrace our authentic selves with vigor and become transparent as much as possible to our self, to our family and friends, and to our community. It is through the letting go of masks and the illuminating of our shadows that we can truly move forward as 'new men' into this new stage of our lives and become abundant and spiritual Elders. Without confronting our shadows and recognizing their presence often as motivation for our behaviors, we are unable to become generative, to mentor with integrity, and to bless with authenticity.

The shadow is represented in the legend of Parsifal by the Red Knight. Parsifal must kill the Red Knight and take his armor in order to take on his passionate manhood.

Shadows and shadowy behavior often began in childhood when we found ourselves in situations that caused us to take on defensive postures and survival roles. When we were born, we were born with a natural buoyancy, positive self-esteem, and feeling of well-being. This is often referred to as the "Golden Child." Over time, we might have received negative messages from parents, siblings and, later on, teachers, coaches, and friends. We might have lost that buoyancy and love for life as voices in our heads said to us that we are not good enough, that we ought to be perfect, we ought to be like someone else, we are not wanted, and other negative scripts. If we were born into a family suffering a crisis or trauma (examples: someone addicted to drugs or alcohol, someone suffering from cancer or other chronic disease, a death of a parent or child, someone with mental illness) we might have taken on roles that, at the time, protected us or helped us survive the trauma. We might have put on a persona, or mask, that we showed to the world and hid our real self.

These roles and scripts we play over and over, which once worked, often become false selves and masks. Often, our behavior is driven by these patterns, especially when events become tense and stressful. We try again and again to use behaviors that once worked but now become inauthentic, unconscious responses. These roles might include the Victim who in one way or another feels put down, weak, victimized. One might feel deserving of a less than vibrant life, accepting life's downturns, and unable to function vitally in interactions with others. Others might use arrogance and bullying behaviors to get their way. Some appear to be driven to isolation and lone wolf behaviors. Many stay in their heads, attempting to control and manipulate. All of these shadowy behaviors have the effect of damaging and destroying relationships, with one's authentic self, with those we love, and with acquaintances and fellow employees.

Without fluidity, creativity, the courage to face one's self and one's shadows, as was the case of the older brothers in the story *The Water of Life*, one might feel trapped, frustrated and at a loss as to why one fails to get what most individuals want: intimacy with loved ones, fulfilling work, positive and valued friendships, and the fulfillment of one's most cherished goals and dreams.

Shadowy behavior relates directly with the drive to build one's ego. As Jung suggested, the first half of life is generally focused on developing a healthy ego that often defends and protects the wounded self within. The driving force is usually inward and centered on accomplishment, developing wealth, making impressive purchases, comparing oneself against others, culturally generated and acceptable marks of achievement, winning and losing, and impressing others.

Yet, deep under the mask and beneath the script and role, lives our authentic self, what some psychologists call the "golden child" or "inner child." With personal work, the feedback and support of others, and a willingness to move from self-centered to other-centered goals (intimate connection to others, believing in abundance and from that place of abundance – time, treasure and talent – honoring, blessing, supporting, inspiring others, especially the next generation) one can become generative, deeply spiritual and valued. This is the goal of the second half of life and of the Vibrant Emeritus.

For many men, the journey to transcendence and transformation is difficult. With a culture charged with the energy of youth, with few role models, and without clear maps and directions many men end up staying stuck in their first half of life strategies, and wonder why they feel so unfulfilled as ego-centered goals become less satisfying and meaningful.

Recognizing and detecting our shadows, looking at their

sources, moving them out of our subconscious and bringing them out of the darkness into the light we can manage our behavior, and with work and time we can embrace and live from our truest, most honorable and ennobling selves that live deeply within us all.

A Classic Tale

The Prince and the Portrait
(Based on Oscar Wilde's *The Picture of Dorian Gray*)
Once upon a time, in the days of magical objects, in a kingdom by the sea a Prince was born. The Prince grew into an unusually beautiful youth, raised mostly by his mother. His father, the King, was often absent with the affairs of state and in faraway wars to protect his kingdom. The Queen cuddled the Prince as he grew. He could do no wrong. The people fell in love with such a beautiful boy. As a youth, his face grew luminous. He walked with grace. His body grew strong and he had great athletic prowess.

When he was eighteen, the King commanded that the boy come to him for inspection.

"Yes," thought the King, "I have done well to have produced such a son."

The King commanded that there be a statewide party for the son. He called for his court Magician.

"I want my son to be given a present that will serve him all his life that no other Prince can match."

The Magician traveled far and wide but could not find such a unique gift. At last he traveled deep in the forest where he found a beautiful woman playing a harp. She sang an enchanting song. Outside a girl child played.

The Magician told the woman his plight.

"Do not worry, I will help you. Have the court painter make a portrait of the Prince."

The Magician returned to the castle and to the painter.

Knowing the importance of this painting, the painter exhausted himself drawing, sketching and finally painting his masterpiece. The moment he finished, he dropped dead. Meanwhile, the enchantress slipped into the studio and cast a spell.

At the party everyone was amazed by the portrait – it almost appeared alive.

On the day after the party, the King departed again for foreign lands. The Queen went about her business as though nothing had changed. But deep in the heart of the Prince, a longing stirred. Before leaving, the Prince took a last look at the picture. He noticed a change in the face. The mouth was drawn into a smirk and the eyes betrayed wanderlust. The Prince put the portrait into an inner chamber and locked the room for which he held the only key. Quietly he left the castle.

The Prince roamed far and wide seeking to fulfill his longing. He spent most of his days in low places, learning the ways of drunkenness, debauchery and desire.

On the occasion that he returned to the castle and looked at the portrait, he found that picture now portrayed an individual he could hardly recognize as himself, so deformed and grotesque it had become.

Those who looked upon the face of the Prince were amazed that he hadn't seemed to age since the night of his eighteenth birthday party.

Rumors of his debauchery spread, lives ruined, gambling debts unpaid, reckless living, but who could believe such rumors when looking upon the visage of resplendent youth?

One day the Prince wandered into the forest. He heard the voice of a young woman. Called to her, he was entranced. He vowed to end his debauched ways to be worthy of the purity he perceived in her.

A year passed in which he lived entirely morally. Before he

reentered the forest to find the young woman of his dreams, he went to his portrait to see if it had changed back. He was shocked to find it even more grotesque.

Realizing that his 'self-sacrifice' was motivated by self-interest, and the quest for new emotional experience, the Prince decided that only a full confession would absolve him. He pulled his sword and plunged it into the canvas.

Outside the servants heard a bloodcurdling cry. They rushed to the portrait chamber and found the grotesque body of the prince recognizable only by the rings on his fingers; his sword plunged deep into his heart.

Some Questions You Might Reflect Upon:

The masks we wear often begin as survival roles and strategies. Especially in families where there is a deep wound – addictive behavior, mental illness, cancer, violence – members of the family often begin wearing masks so that the family secret is hidden from those outside the family. Certainly, the Prince in the story makes his visage a mask hiding his base desires. Perhaps his mask began when his father abandoned him and his mother coddled him, neither parent an authentic mother or father. How might you and your immediate family members have put on masks to hide a secret – your own secret or a family member?

When the Prince desires to be authentic, he finds that he has forgotten how – lying to himself as well as the woman he loves. How difficult might it be for you to release your mask and be authentic to those you love and with whom you want real relationships?

Ultimately, his inability to be authentic costs the Prince his life. What is hanging onto masks and survival roles costing you?

A Contemporary Story: My Shadows

If shadows begin in childhood wounds, as I believe they do, mine begin with the shadowy parenting behavior of my parents. When my father was dying he described his 55-year marriage as "two misfits who had no idea what they were doing." My father felt guilty all his life for leaving his family during the Depression to go on his youthful adventures as a Marine during World War II. He had a genius IQ. He had very little role-model fathering from his father who was reclusive and distant. My mother was the daughter of a man who abandoned my grandmother. Her father owned a railroad and provided my mother with a home in Massachusetts, a winter home in Florida with free passage on the railroads, a university education at Duke University, but no connection to him. Both my parents had little confidence in themselves, even though both had amazing skills and talents.

My mother at 88 is still highly controlling, and she dominated and psychologically abused me for many years. I still have dreams of Medusa with the face of my mother. My father never protected me from my mother. He is faceless in my dreams.

When I was three years old, my parents moved to my great-grandfather's house in Louisville. We lived in two bedrooms on the second floor sharing the kitchen. One bedroom was our living room. The other was our bedroom. I slept in my parents' bedroom until I was ten years old. When I was ten, my mother took a job as a teacher at the Catholic school I attended. I was the only kid who brought his mother to school. I was with my mother all day every day until I went to high school. She insisted on tutoring me every night until I graduated. She controlled my wardrobe. When I was ready for college, I had no choice but to go to Duke. At Duke I received advice letters several times a week. I tossed them into the garbage can at the post office.

My dad never seemed quite able to connect with other men. He was mostly in his head. I often fantasized about being the son of my friends' dads, and longed to have a dad who was passionate about sport teams, was physically active, and who would take me into his confidence and tell me the secrets I hallucinated fathers tell their sons. I became completely inept around other boys on my team, never getting the jokes they told to each other or understanding the secrets they seemed to know among themselves about girls and sex and the lore of boys. I was a better than average athlete, but chose sports like tennis where I could depend on myself and perform in isolation.

My dad wrote the checks to enable my mother's fantasies. About a year before he died, he confessed to me that he was over $100,000 in debt even after spending his working years as a financial officer and advisor. My mother wanted to go on trips to Europe and Hawaii and buy expensive new cars. He could not deny her.

I thought this was normal in families.

What I noticed about my friends' families were warm and loving mothers who often hugged their sons, and dads who involved their sons in sports and traditionally male activities. None of this happened in my house. There was no physical expression of love between my parents, no hugs or kisses. I was seldom touched. To get what she wanted from me, my mother lied to me, manipulated me, and went behind my back to get what she wanted. My father seemed to allow this to happen.

My work as a man has been to face these shadows and work on my behaviors driven by my shadows. For many years I lived with a deep rage at my father for perceived weaknesses as a man and as my father. It was hard for me to trust women. Having no siblings, I tried to create family by making friends into my brothers and sisters. I often prefer isolation rather than relating to others, my wife, my children, my friends, even though I completely love and trust those dearest to me.

The mask I wear as a Lover is the Nice Guy. Behind the mask is the one who will do anything to be liked. Love me, love me. I will be totally co-dependent and let you walk all over me.

The mask I wear as a Warrior is the self-sufficient one. Behind the mask is one who can do it all on his own, doesn't trust anyone, who doesn't need allies, the Lone Ranger, who doesn't connect and can be a loose cannon.

The mask I wear as a Magician is the expert others seek out for advice. Behind the mask is the one who is the master manipulator, duplicitous, sneaky, the Evil Vizier. I have learned many techniques to hypnotize, impress and control others.

The mask I wear as the King is benevolent ruler. Behind the mask is the one who lets his kingdom become a wasteland, focused on his wounds, resentful, waiting to be healed by others, but never asking for love and support.

As I enter my Elder years, my work is to loosen these masks, allow others to see who I am, be transparent, and become congruent, my outside reflecting my loving, benevolent soul, letting my Golden Child breathe and live close to the surface.

Discussion

Our shadows are what we hide, repress and deny; the ugliness we don't want others to see. But repressed and pushed down, they often drive the bus of our behaviors. In the story of *The Prince and the Portrait*, the king is aloof and away from his son, and the queen cuddles him. Neither are very good role models or parents. The king seeks a magic gift and the Magician produces a portrait that shows the wantonness of the prince's life as he seeks for meaning aimlessly. He appears to be searching for his core, but does not know how or where to seek. At last, when he wants to be authentic, he finds even this is a con to get what he wants. His death comes in a last and final combat with himself, a ritual suicide, and the shadows of his life overcoming him.

Without self-confrontation, hiding behind the masks we construct, like the prince we can live our lives driven by self-deceit, unquestioned projections, engaged in inauthenticity, all the while pretending to be the opposite. No personal growth is possible until one courageously looks at one's shadows, keeps them in one's consciousness, and changes one's behavior. Over and over one might find one behaving out of one's shadow. If others around one are willing to give feedback on the effect of one's behavior, then it is possible to look at the behavior and chose a different path.

Robert Moore, in his book *King, Warrior, Magician, Lover*, suggests that in our young life, we men begin by seeking to be Warriors. We are often attracted to the energy of men who set boundaries, take a stand, draw a line in the sand, and protect others. We can also be attracted to the shadow Warrior who gets his way from using force, seeks to win even by cutting corners or taking advantage of others, and dominates without personal boundaries. Later, many men combine the Warrior energy with the Magician. The Magician represents ingenuity, figuring things out, and the ability to compete intellectually. Shadow Magician energy includes being tricky, figuring the angles, taking advantage through manipulation. Magician energy allows the Warrior to build a career.

As we age, we include the Lover as we build relationships. These might include partners and spouses, business relationships, friends we hang out with, and relationships with our children and family. Acting out of the shadow Lover can include becoming addicted to pleasures, other people, and life as it is.

In our early adult years, especially when one is actively building one's life, one's career and one's family, the combination of Warrior, Magician and Lover work well, especially if one is conscious of the shadow energies and selects to stay in the positive energy of each archetype.

As we age, however, many men get stuck in this confluence without stepping further and embracing the energy of the King. King energy relies on deepening one's spirituality, depth as a man, willingness to step into true vision and wisdom, and ruling the other archetypes with balance. Men who age unconsciously are in danger of becoming tyrants, raging about the inequities of their life journeys, and fail to become beneficent, blessing, giving and wise.

Challenges

Challenge One: Writing Your Story

1. Reflect on the classic tale of *The Prince and the Portrait* and think about its themes, its use of archetypes, and its perspectives on growth, change, and healing.
2. Reflect on the contemporary story and how it connects with the classic tale.
3. Reflect on your own shadows, especially about aging, and write your own contemporary story.

Challenge Two: Shadow Visualization

1. Either read the following visualization into a recorder so that you can play it to yourself or ask a person you trust to read it to you. Make sure to pause for ten seconds between each line.
2. Place a notebook or journal next to you with your favorite pen.
3. Playing soft, meditative music can enhance the experience.
4. Follow the direction of the visualization narrative:

I invite you to lie down on your back in a place where you feel alone,
Just relax and breathe deeply
A deep cleansing breath
Take a deep breath through your nose and
Hold it

And let it go slowly out your mouth
(Do this 3 more times)
And now as you relax and breathe normally concentrate on
    the breath as it enters and leaves your nostrils
Just at the place where the breath comes and goes
Until you are completely relaxed
Your neck and shoulders relaxed
Let go of any tension there
Let go
Of any tension in your core, your belly and lower back, just
    relax
Let go
Of any tension in your hips, your thighs, just relax
Let go
Of any tension in your calves, your knees
Let go
Of any tension in your ankles and feet
Just relax and concentrate on your breath
Coming and going, coming and going
Gradually you find yourself on a path
The path winds into the woods and down
Down, down a long path that switches back and forth
You are going deeper and deeper down toward a river
A river that flows deep down to where the path comes beside
    it
So you walk along the river on the path
The trees of the woods grow all the way down to the river
The river flows steadily forward along the path
You walk along the river until you come to a boat on the bank
You step into the boat as you push the boat into the water
You lie back in the boat and feel the motion of the river
You move at a gentle rate and above you see the tall trees of
    the woods
After a while, you can no longer see the sky as the canopy

above you thickens

The river moves you onward until a branch of the river moves you toward a cave entry

The boat glides you into the dark cave, so dark that you can no longer see even your hand before your eyes

Moving deeper into the cave, you begin to see the flickering of a fire against the rock walls of the cave

And as you go deeper, the shadows on the walls grow longer and higher up the walls

The shadows on the walls remind you of a time when you were sad and you did not like feeling sad

The shadows remind you of times long ago when you were frightened by what was happening around you and you wanted to be protected

Wanting to be protected you may have found a way

Maybe you told yourself if I am good enough bad things wouldn't happen

Maybe if I did enough for others they would include me

Maybe if I were perfect I'd please my parents

Maybe if I did only what I was good at others would see me and praise me

Maybe if stayed very still and quiet I'd disappear

Maybe if I was bad enough others would notice me

Maybe if I got really angry no one would mess with me

Maybe if I was funny enough the tension would go away

Maybe if I was silly nothing would be serious

Maybe if I was clever and sly, I could get what I wanted

Maybe if I intimidated you you'd respect me

Maybe if I could make you like me I could get what I want from you

Maybe, maybe, maybe

The fire grows higher and the shadows deepen

You see only what you want to see

If only you were in control of yourself, of others, of the world

Gradually the boat moves on and you leave the shadows in the background

Gradually light comes from another entrance to the cave

You float out of the entrance back under the canopy of trees,

Gradually the light shows through the tops of the trees

Gradually you see the sky

The boat comes to rest on the riverbank

Gradually the boat disappears

You find yourself lying on the floor

Slowly you come back into the room

Taking time to open your eyes,

You look around and sit up

You pick up your favorite pen and begin to write in your notebook or journal

Letting the shadows you discovered come back into consciousness

So that you can write them down, and maybe why they still motivate some of your behaviors.

Challenge Three: What Might be at Risk?

If one is responsive to one's inner calling to be an Elder, one almost immediately finds oneself with the dilemma of facing one's shadows and the self-imposed reluctance to not let go of one's ego-based first half of life goals. We often envision risks to ourselves that lurk if we were to let go so that we might embrace an abundant and blessing Elder life. Here are a set of questions you might want to examine, face and answer in order for you to consider letting go and making a clear change in your lifestyle, purpose and search for meaning:

What might be at risk for you to accept your life as an Elder?

What might be at risk if you let go of your Hero/Warrior life of acquisition, seeking the honors of achievement, and continuous ego building?

What might be at risk for you to take care of yourself physically?
What might be at risk for you to go deeper into your masculine spirituality?
What fears come up when you contemplate aging?
What might happen if you continue on the course you are presently following?
What is at risk for you to make changes in your life?
Do you ever find yourself deep in the woods without a direction? What might be at risk for you to move forward and embrace a new calling?

1. Find someone you deeply trust to work with who might also be asking himself similar questions. Use all of the above questions or select the one or ones that speak to you most deeply as prompts for you to begin to embrace as a Vibrant Emeritus.
2. One partner asks each question, repeats if necessary, takes notes of the answers, and decides when the other partner has given a deep 'truth response.'
3. Once one has given a 'truth response' i.e. a response that seems to come most deeply from the heart and comes most closely to the true nature of the resistance to not moving forward, the partners switch roles.
4. Only one question is given per round.
5. When all the selected questions are answered, ask each other: "What will it take for you to overcome this resistance?"

Challenge Four: The Masks I Wear

Jungian psychologists Douglas Gillette and Robert Moore describe four archetypes of the mature male. Each of the archetypes has both a bright golden side and a shadow. For mature men who are ready to move into a Vibrant Emeritus status, recognizing the shadow of each archetype and how it appears in their own personality can be a huge step toward embracing themselves as blessing and mentoring Elders.

(For a deeper and more complex description, go to the original source: Gillette and Moore's *King, Warrior, Magician, Lover: Rediscovering the Archetypes of the Mature Masculine.*)

Read and examine each of the archetypes:

The Archetype of the King

In the story of Parsifal retold above, Parsifal asks the crucial grail question "Whom do you serve?" and becomes the Grail King. As soon as he utters this question, the deeply wounded Fisher King is healed, the wasteland that had enveloped the Grail Castle at once explodes into verdant abundance, peace and justice reigns in the castle, and the people are happy.

When the King is wounded, only desert wasteland appears, the land is filled with aimless violence, knights and Warriors are needed to keep peace and mete out justice, and the people live miserable lives. In our psyche, if our King is weak or wounded, we and those we love suffer. The King is our core; and without strong King energy within, chaos rules our person and disharmony rules our life.

When the King is healthy, vibrant, and strong, he is bestows blessings on his kingdom, is a source of wisdom, strong character, and integrity. He is beloved by his people, his lands flourish, and his loved ones honor, respect and bless him.

The shadow side of the King is the Tyrant. Quite often, mature men who do not embrace their Vibrant Emeritus status continue to stay in their Warrior lives attempting to relive their glory years, hang on to power, set up impenetrable borders around themselves, and attempt to continue the life of competition and trophy collection. If their lives become empty and their purposes meaningless, men can fall into the depletion and wasting they so feared by many men contemplating their Elder years.

When the Elder wears the mask of the King as a survival role, he often attempts to hide the shadow of the Tyrant within.

When the loving and benevolent King shows his authentic soul, he, those he loves, and the inner kingdom flourish.

The Archetype of the Warrior

Parsifal is, of course, as the hero of his legend, the greatest knight in the court. He defeats the Red Knight and wears the defeated knight's armor over his homespun garments, symbols of his innocence and purity. The Red Knight is the only knight he kills. Instead he sends defeated knights to the King where they pledge their fealty to the King and pledge their lives to defending the weak and defenseless. The Warrior phase of Parsifal's legend lasts for many years, until he has accomplished his Warrior purpose and is ready to reenter the Grail Castle, embrace his Elderhood, and become the Grail King.

When the knight/Warrior is ruled by a strong King, he performs brilliantly, setting and defending boundaries, protecting the weak and defenseless including his own inner child, meting out justice, saving damsels, and slaying dragons. The Warrior is highly energetic, bears deep pain, follows an adventure until its conclusion, and offers those he defeats peace and justice.

It is the Warrior energy in one's psyche who is the doer, building the skills he needs to complete his mission in life. He is able to battle adversaries and obstacles that hinder his pursuit of his life goals. He takes on responsibility and lives a life of integrity.

The shadow of the Warrior is the cruel sadist. A rogue adventurer who serves no king, the shadow Warrior takes what he wants regardless of the consequence to others. He obeys no code of honor or integrity. His family suffers abandonment to his personal desires. Or, turning in on himself, the shadow Warrior inflicts his own savage energy on himself, becoming the victim, that is, the one who is helpless and cannot muster the energy to engage his Warrior status.

Men often wear the mask of the vital Warrior to hide either the sadist or masochist within.

The Archetype of the Magician

The archetype of the Magician first appears in the Parsifal legend in the form of his mentor Gournamond. Gournamond takes the uneducated and naive young man under his protection and teaches him the arts of the Warrior, connects him to his spirituality and his mission – the procurement of the Grail and the healing of the land – and helps him to form his full masculinity.

The Magician energy in the male is the energy of rationality, of figuring things out, of solving problems, of using strategy, and of tapping into our spiritual strength and personal magic. The Magician is the tactician, the thinker, the analyst, the planner and the motivator.

Parsifal applies all that his mentor has taught him and connects it with his youthful ideals and dreams. Parsifal was raised deep in the forest, symbol of the magical and mysterious. One can imagine the only child lying on the soft grass at night looking up at the stars. Even as a knight he wears the homespun clothes from this time in his life, so he is able to tap into the energy of innocence and youth that allows him to enter the Grail Castle and, on his second visit, ask the question: "Whom do you serve?"

The shadow of the Magician is the manipulator, the self-aggrandizer, the one who uses his wiles to dominate and control others.

Men often wear the mask of the superior thinker, the counselor, the advisor to hide self-serving manipulation of others.

The Archetype of the Lover

Parsifal is reared deep in the forest in the heart of mystery and the magical. He is kept innocent and unaware of the ways of men by his mother. Yet, when he encounters the five knights whom he takes as demigods, his blood is stirred and he passionately leaves his mother for the path of adventure. On his way to the King, he encounters a woman who stirs his deep feeling for love. Quixotically, he challenges the Red Knight and slays him. The knight's page has to instruct him on how to wear his armor over his homespun clothes, yet it is Parsifal as the fool who ultimately is crowned the Grail King.

The Lover energy in men is passion, the one who is called into passionate service. The Lover leads with his heart and connects to his inner spirit. Lover energy connects with the hearts of others. The Lover resists convention, standards, structure and order. The Lover offers the benefits of the humane, the soulful and love to the other archetypes.

The shadow Lover is the addict, the one who is overcome by pleasure, sets no boundaries to self-gratifications, endlessly searches for meaning without knowing where to seek, and exhausts himself with unmeasured passion.

The mask the Lover wears is often that of one's zest for life, hiding depression, wasting, and constant pleasure seeker. Follow these instructions:

1. Reread the shadows for each archetype.
2. Take four pieces of copy paper and a small bowl that comes close to filling the page.
3. Draw the circular outline on each piece of paper.
4. Cut out the circle from each piece of paper.
5. At the top of each circle, write the name in bold letters of one of each of the archetypes.
6. On the side with the name of the archetype, write words and phrases or draw pictures that indicate the mask you show to the world that you want others to see you as a King, Warrior, Magician, or Lover.
7. On the other side write words and phrases or draw pictures that reveal the shadow King, Warrior, Magician or Lover.
8. With a trusted person, who also wishes to do these exercises, talk one at a time about each side for each archetype.
9. Discuss with your partner how you might want to work with your shadows and masks to become more transparent and authentic.

A Poem to Contemplate

In the Old Age of the Soul
By Ezra Pound

I do not choose to dream; there cometh on me
Some strange old lust for deeds
As to the nerveless hand of some old warrior
The sword-hilt or the war-worn wonted helmet
Brings momentary life and long-fled cunning,
So to my soul grown old –
Grown old with many a jousting, many a foray,
Grown old with many a hither-coming and hence-going –
Till now they send him dreams and no more deed;
So doth he flame again with might for action,
Forgetful of the council of elders,
Forgetful that who rules doth no more battle,
Forgetful that such might no more cleaves to him
So doth he flame again toward valiant doing.

Some Questions to Reflect Upon:

How might clinging to one's Hero years be shadow driven?

Must cunning and strength leave the aging man?

How might this poem represent being stuck in the Hero years?

Is weariness a shadow?

Practice

Embracing the Shadow
In her book *The Second Half of Life: Opening the Eight Gates of*

Wisdom, cultural anthropologist Angeles Arrien suggests the practice of using David Richo's series of "Practices of Befriending the Shadow," taken from his book: *Shadow Dance: Liberating the Power and Creativity of Your Dark Side:*

Can I be committed to a relationship... While still remaining free?

Can I be angry at someone... While loving toward this person?

Can I be aware of my faults... While high in self-esteem?

Can I be against an idea or plan... While respectful and cooperative?

Can I be in agreement... While still firm in my own convictions?

Can I be respectful and yielding... While still firm in my own beliefs?

Can I be a preserver of what is useful in a belief system... While still free to discard what no longer works for me?

Can I be a parent or spouse... While still being true to a career or hobby?

Can I be repelled by what someone does... While still caring about the one who did it?

Can I be generous... While still being self-nurturing?

Can I be emotionally involved... While still being intellectually clear?

Can I be proud of someone... While still being aware of the person's shortcomings?

Can I be available for others... While still being able to preserve time for myself?

Can I be flexible... While still being true to my standards?

Can I be able to see the worst possibilities... While still being hopeful?

Can I be able to take risks... While still being safety conscious?

Can I be responsibly in control of myself... While still being spontaneous?

Can I be limited in my commitment... While still being unconditionally loving?

Can I be afraid... While still being capable of acting?

Can I be honest in my personal life... While still working on my shadow?

To use this practice, one might select one question each day. If using a journal, one might enter one's reflections as one considers the tension of each opposing element. What might be one's conclusion for each question?

Growth Questions

Discuss the following questions with a friend or consider what they evoke in you in a journal:

How difficult is it for me to honestly look at myself?

Shadow work is, indeed, work. What's at risk for me to let go and do this work?

What is the worst that might happen if I let go and tell the truth about myself to trusted friends or individuals in a confidential support group?

What might I gain from facing shadows?

Have I had the experience of opening up and finding that others validated me and my experience?

Have I had the experience of learning that others carry the same shadows, face the same problems and have the same fears that I do? If so, was that freeing for me?

What ongoing practice might I consider for continuing my healthy shadow work?

Chapter 4

Standing at the Crossroads

*I come to a crossroads. It is late and I am chilly. Which one will I
choose? What will I need for the road? Am I enough?*
This is the third task.

And so here we stand, together at the crossroads in the midst
of life with the artists, wunderkinds, and kings, gazing Janus-
like forward and back, trying to figure out what the rest of our
days on earth will bring. Trying to formulate a strategy. Trying
to discover where the gold of happiness and fulfillment lies
hidden. Trying to find out if there really is any gold.

And then that little voice comes again: Time is running out.
Is this really all there is?

– Harry R. Moody, *The Five Stages of the Soul*

The Task: Standing at the Crossroads

Having honored and reflected on one's accomplishments and
come to the realization that continuing the heroic Warrior life
may lead to empty action or meaningless accolades (another
cruise, a bigger house, more golf, building another business) one
comes to a crossroads. Many men have the greatest difficulty
here. Perhaps one has been a 'taker' all one's Warrior years, and
shifting gears to becoming a 'giver' can be daunting. Letting go of
action that leads to personal reward to action that empowers and
blesses might feel counterintuitive. One's shadows around aging
will appear again and again as motivators of ineffective response
if we do not keep them before us and visible. And it is here that
the great decision comes to move forward and embrace a vibrant
second life or stay at a standstill, looking back and fearful of the
future. Will one take on the challenge of self-transcendence?

Michael Meade writes in *Men and the Water of Life*:

A man can get caught between an outer life whose meaning is draining away and an inner life dominated by lions enraged from lack of nourishment. After a while, stuckness becomes numbing – one of the most fearful states men experience. Turning numb happens in all kinds of ways and has become so common that it's considered part of aging. Certainly, it is one of our fears about aging. Whatever the primary emotional style of a man may be, numbing can occur. His anger may turn cold and form a hard shell that blocks his inner and outer life. Even a warm heart may become stone cold and kill intimacy of any kind. Fear may become petrified, keeping people at a distance and blocking change within. Shame may build to a point where any close attention will shut everything down; it can stop a man from doing something before he even gets started. Sorrow may begin to feel like a weight that can't be moved, and a wasteland can grow out of the numbness.

In the present culture, because of the dearth of role models, honored and respected Elders in our lives, and the dearth of men who see Elderhood as anything but a depressing vision of life of debilitation, we often get stuck at the crossroads where a decision is called for. I have met many men who appear confused about what to do with their lives as they age and their careers are ending. Life as a Vibrant Emeritus can be as active, challenging, growing and exciting as life as a Warrior. It is life on a different frequency and it is emitting energy out to others from one's deepest core. I have met men whose confusion comes from their attempt to continue to do what they have always done to stoke and stroke their inner dynamism, and it is no longer working. I talked with others who have lost their purpose.

Life as a Vibrant Emeritus offers the discovery of new

challenges that can be met in ways that demand creativity, movement into what is unknown, "going we know not where to fetch we know not what." Men taking this route today are pioneers and early adapters, forging the path others will want to follow. We will become the role models, supporters and inspirers for the next generations, mentoring them through their Warrior Journey, and lowering the obstacles to their entering the last half or third of their lives with passion, enthusiasm and joy.

Parsifal reached this point when he had saved enough damsels, killed enough dragons and done enough noble deeds. He comes to his crossroads when he meets the old man fishing and stops to fish with him. His decision is to reenter the Grail Castle, the castle of adult male spirituality where transformation, self-transcendence, and altered consciousness can happen. This time Parsifal is man enough to pay attention, understand the symbols and ask the right question about service to others. In so doing, he takes on his Vibrant Emeritus status as Grail King, the vibrations of his soul so great that they cure and make abundant an entire kingdom.

The task here is very much a matter of reversing the commonly held beliefs, the usual opinions, and the negative perspective on aging held within our self, our communities and our culture. Recently, new perspectives about aging are beginning to come into the field of this culture as evidenced by the books, websites, and resources listing in the References of this book and are becoming known as the "new aging." Typical with the 'Baby Boomers' is a focus on our experience as it is happening. For some of us, we hold the terror that change often evokes. For others, it is the exhilaration of taking on a challenge first. For me there is always both terror and exhilaration when moving into terra incognito, or at sea moving toward unknown shores.

What many Boomers have is the experience of challenging boundaries throughout our youth. This includes both challenging the Vietnam War and having the courage to fight for one's country. Included is willingness to experiment and use conscious changing drugs and for some to face one's own addiction. Also included is youthful embracing of idealism, vision and a change-the-world philosophy. Many commentators have noted that the Boomers lost the idealism of their youth as they built self-serving lives of avarice, ruthless commerce and self-obsessiveness. My belief is that alive under those shadows lives our better consciousness. Boomers have the opportunity to reconnect with their better selves and inhabit the noble goals of youth merged with the practical skills, understandings and know-how they gained as Warriors. My hope is that many of them will have the courage to do so.

A Classic Tale

Go I Know Not Whither, to Fetch I Know Not What
(A Russian Fairy Tale)
By the blue sea, in a certain empire, there dwelt once upon a time a king who was a bachelor, and he had a whole company of archers, and the archers used to go a-hunting with him and shoot the birds that flew about, and provided meat for their master's table. In this company served a youthful archer named Fedot, a clever marksman was he, never missing his aim, wherefore the King loved him better than all his comrades.

One day he chanced to go a-hunting very early, even at break of day. He went into a dense, drear forest, and there he saw a dove sitting on a tree. Fedot stretched his bow, took aim, fired and broke one of the dove's little wings, and the bird fell from the tree down upon the damp earth. The marksman picked it up, and was about to twist its neck and put it in his pouch, when the dove thus spoke to him:

"Alas! young marksman! do not twist my poor little silly neck; drive me not out of the white world. 'Twere better to take me alive, carry me home, put me in thy little window, and lo! the moment that slumber comes over me, at that very moment, I say, stroke me the wrong side down with thy right hand, and great good fortune shall be thine!"

The marksman was much amazed.

"Why, what is this?" thought he. "Mine eyes tell me 'tis a bird, and naught else, yet it speaks with a human voice! Such a thing has never happened to me before."

So he took the bird home, placed it in the windowsill, and waited and waited. 'Twas not very long before the bird laid its head beneath its wing and began to doze. Then the marksman raised his right hand and stroked it, quite lightly, the wrong side down. The dove instantly fell to the ground and became a maiden-soul, and so beautiful that the like of it can only be told in tales, but is neither to be imagined nor guessed at.

And she spoke to the good youth, who was the royal archer, and said: "Thou hast had wit enough to win me, have also wit enough to live with me. Thou art my predestined husband, I am thy preordained wife."

They were immediately of one mind. Fedot married, lived at home, and rejoiced in his young wife, yet forgot not his service either. Every morning, before break of day, he took his weapon, went into the forest, shot various kinds of wild beasts, and took them to the royal kitchen. But it was plain that his wife was much tormented by these hunting expeditions, and one day she said to him:

"Listen, my friend! I am fearful for thee! Every blessed day thou dost cast thyself into the forest, dost wander through fen and morass, and returnest home wet through and through, and we are none the better for it. What sort of a trade dost thou call this! Look now, I have a plan whereby thou also shalt profit by it. Get me now a hundred or two of rubles, and I'll manage all the rest."

Then Fedot hastened to his comrades, and borrowed a ruble

from one, and two rubles from another till he had collected about two hundred rubles. These then he brought to his wife.

"Now," said she, "buy me various kinds of silk with all this money!"

The archer went and bought various kinds of silk with the two hundred rubles.

She took them and said: "Be not sorrowful! Pray God and lay thee down to sleep, the morning is wiser than the evening!"

So the husband fell asleep, and the wife went out upon the balcony, opened her book of spells, and immediately two invisible youths appeared before her and said:

"What art thou pleased to command?"

"Take this silk, and in a single hour weave me a carpet more wondrous than anything to be found in the wide world, and let the whole kingdom be embroidered on this carpet, with all its cities and villages and rivers and lakes."

Then they set to work and wove the carpet, and it was wondrous to behold, wondrous above everything. In the morning the wife handed the carpet to her husband.

"There," said she, "take it to the marketplace and sell it to the merchants; but look now! haggle not about the price, but take whatever they offer thee for it."

Fedot took the carpet, turned it round, hung it over his arm, and went to the marketplace. A merchant saw him, ran up to him at once, and said to him: "Hearken to me, honoured sir, wilt thou not sell me that carpet?"

"Willingly!"

"And what then is the price?"

"Thou art a frequenter of the marts, therefore will I leave the price to thee!"

The merchant fell a-thinking and a-thinking. He could not price the carpet. He was at his wits' end. Another merchant came running up, and after him a third and a fourth till a great crowd of them collected; they looked at the carpet, marvelled at it, and could not fix the price. At that moment the royal steward passed by that way, saw the crowd, and wanted to know what all the merchants were talking about. So he went up to them and said, "What is the matter?"

"We cannot price this carpet," said they. The steward looked at the carpet, and he also was amazed.

"Hearken, archer!" said he, "tell me the real truth; where didst thou get this lordly carpet?"

"My wife wrought it!"

"How much dost thou want for it?"

"I myself know not the value of it; my wife bade me not to haggle over it, but to take whatever was offered."

"Then what dost thou say to 10,000 rubles?"

The archer took the money and gave up the carpet. Now this steward was always by the King, and ate and drank at his table. So he went to dine with the King now also, and took the carpet with him.

"Would it please your Majesty to look at the carpet I have bought to-day?" The King looked, and saw there his whole realm just as if it were on the palm of his hand, and he heaved a great sigh. "Why, what a carpet is this! In all my life I have never seen such cunning craft. Say now, what wilt thou take for this carpet?"

And the King drew out 25,000 rubles and gave them into the hand of the steward, but the carpet they hung up in the palace.

"That is a mere nothing," thought the steward, "I'll make a much better thing out of the second chance."

So he immediately went in search of the archer, sought out his little hut, entered the dwelling-room, and the moment he saw the archer's wife, at that very instant he forgot all about himself and the errand on which he had come. Nevertheless the steward manned himself with a great effort and turned sullenly homewards. From henceforth he bungled over everything he took in hand, and whether asleep or awake, he thought only of one thing, the wonderfully lovely little archeress.

The King observed the change in him, and asked him, "What ails thee? Has any great grief befallen thee?"

"Alas! my king and father, I have seen the wife of the archer; such a beauty the world knows not of nor has ever seen!"

The King himself was seized with a desire to fall in love with her, and he also went to the abode of the archer. He entered the living-room, and saw before him a lady of a loveliness unspeakable.

"Why should I remain a bachelor any longer?" thought he. "Lo! now, I'll marry this beauty, she's too good for a mere archer. From her birth she was evidently meant to be a Queen!"

The King returned to his palace and said to the steward, "Hearken! thou hast had wit enough to show me the archer's wife, that unspeakable beauty; thou must now have wit enough to remove the husband out of the way. I want to marry her myself. And if thou dost not remove him, look to thyself; although thou art my faithful servant, thou shalt be hanged upon a gallows!"

Then the steward went about much more afflicted than before, and think as he would, he could not devise a method of getting rid of the archer. He wandered about the broad market-places and the narrow lanes, and there met him one day a miserable old hag.

"Stay, thou King's servant!" cried she. "I can see all thy thoughts, thou wantest help against thy unavoidable woe."

"Ah, help me, dear little granny! I'll pay thee what thou wilt!"

"Thou hast received the royal command to get rid of Fedot the archer. The thing is not so very easy. He indeed is simple, but his wife is frightfully artful. Well now, we'll hit upon an errand which will not be accomplished so speedily. Go to the King and say that he must command the archer to go I know not whither, and fetch I know not what. Such a task as that he'll never accomplish, though he live for ever and ever; either he will vanish out of knowledge altogether, or if he does come back, it will be without arms or legs."

The steward rewarded the old hag with gold, and hastened back to the King, and the King sent and commanded the archer to be brought before him.

"Well, Fedot! thou art my young warrior, and the first in my corps of archers. Render me then this service: Go I know not whither, and fetch me I know not what! And mark me, if thou bring it me not back, 'tis I, the King, who say it to thee, thy head shall be severed from thy shoulders."

The archer turned to the left, quitted the palace, and came home very sad and thoughtful.

His wife asked him: "Why art thou so sorrowful, darling; has any misfortune befallen thee?"

"The King has sent me I know not whither to fetch I know not what. 'Tis through thy beauty that this ruin has come upon us!"

"Yes, indeed! this service is no light one! It takes nine years to get there, and nine years to get back again, eighteen years in all, and God only knows if it can be managed even then!"

"What's to be done then, and what will become of me?"

"Pray God and lie down to sleep, the morning is wiser than the evening. To-morrow thou wilt know all."

The archer lay down to sleep, and his wife sat watching till midnight, opened her book of spells, and the two youths immediately appeared before her.

"What is thy pleasure, and what thy command?"

"Do ye know how one can manage to go I know not whither, and fetch I know not what?"

"No, we do not know." She closed the book, and the youths disappeared from before her eyes. In the morning the archeress awoke her husband.

"Go to the King," said she, "and ask for gold from the treasury for thy journey. Thou hast a pilgrimage of eighteen years before thee. When thou hast the money, come back to me to say farewell."

The archer went to the King, received a whole purseful of money, and returned to say good-bye to his wife.

She gave him a pocket-handkerchief and a ball, and said: "When thou goest out of the town, throw this ball in front of thee, and whithersoever it rolls, follow it. Here too is my pocket-handkerchief; when thou dost wash thyself, wherever thou mayst be, always dry thy face with this handkerchief."

The archer took leave of his wife and of his comrades, bowed low on all four sides of him, and went beyond the barriers of the city. He threw the ball in front of him; the ball rolled and rolled, and he followed hard after it.

A month or so passed away, and then the King called the steward and said to him: "The archer has departed to wander about the wide world for eighteen years, and it is plain that he will not return alive. Now eighteen years are not two weeks, and no little disaster may have befallen him by the way; go then to the archer's house and bring me his wife to the palace!"

So the steward went to the archer's house, entered the room, and said to the beautiful archeress: "Hail, thou wise woman! The King commands thee to present thyself at court!"

So to the court she went. The King received her with joy and led her into his golden halls, and said to her: "Wilt thou be a Queen? I will make thee my spouse!"

"Where was such a thing ever seen, where was such a thing ever heard of, to take a wife away from her living husband? Though he be nothing but a simple archer, he is for all that my lawful husband."

"If thou come not willingly, I'll take thee by force!" But the beauty laughed, stamped upon the floor, turned into a dove, and flew out of the window.

The archer passed through many countries and kingdoms, and the ball kept rolling ever onwards. Whenever they came to a river the ball expanded into a bridge, and whenever the archer wished to rest, the ball widened into a downy bed. Whether the time be long or whether it be short the tale is quickly told, though the deed be not quickly done; suffice it to say that at last the archer came to a vast and wealthy palace; the ball rolled right up against the door and vanished.

The archer fell a-thinking. "I had better go straight on," thought he, so he went up the staircase into a room, and there met him three lovely damsels.

"Whence and wherefore hast thou come hither, good man?"

"Alas! lovely damsels, ye ask me not to rest from my long journey, but ye begin to torment me with questionings. First ye should give me to eat and drink and let me rest, and then only should ye ask me of my tidings!"

They immediately laid the table, gave him to eat and drink, and made him lie down to rest. The archer slept away his weariness, rose from his soft bed, and the lovely damsels brought him a washing-basin and an embroidered towel. He washed himself in the clear spring-water, but the towel he would not take.

"I have my handkerchief wherewith to wipe my face," said he, and he drew out the handkerchief and began to dry himself.

And the lovely damsels fell a-questioning him. "Tell us, good man! whence hast thou got that handkerchief?"

"My wife gave it to me."

"Then thou must have married one of our kinswomen."

Then they called their old mother, and she looked at the handkerchief, recognizing it the same instant, and cried: "This is indeed my daughter's handkerchief!"

Then she began to put all manner of questions to the archer. He told her how he had married her daughter, and how the King had sent him I know not whither, to fetch I know not what.

"Alas! my dear son-in-law, not even I have heard of this marvel. But come now, perchance my servants may know of it."

Then the old woman fetched her book of spells, turned over the leaves, and immediately there appeared two giants.

"What is thy pleasure, and what is thy command?"

"Look now, my faithful servants, carry me together with my son-in-law to the wide sea Ocean, and place us in the very centre of it, in the very abyss."

Immediately the giants caught up the archer and the old woman, and bore them, as by a hurricane, to the wide sea Ocean, and placed them in the centre of it, in the very abyss. There they stood like two vast columns, and held the archer and the old woman in their arms. Then the old woman cried with a loud voice, and there came swimming up to her all the fish and creeping things of the sea, so that the blue sea was no longer to be seen for the multitude of them.

"Hark! ye fishes and creeping things of the sea. Ye who swim everywhere, have ye perchance heard how to go I know not whither, to fetch I know not what?"

And all the fishes and creeping things exclaimed with one voice, "No, we have never heard of it."

Suddenly a lame old croaking frog forced its way to the front and said, "Kwa, kwa; I know where this marvel is to be found."

"Well, dear, that is just what I want to know," said the old woman, and she took up the frog and bade the giants carry her and her son-in-law home. In an instant they found themselves in their own courtyard.

Then the old woman began to question the frog. "How and by what road can my son-in-law go?"

And the frog answered, "This place is at the end of the world, far, far away. I would gladly lead him thither myself, but I am so frightfully old, I can scarcely move my legs. I could not get there in fifty years."

The old woman sent for a big jar, filled it with fresh milk, put the frog inside, and said to her son-in-law, "Hold this jar in thy hand and the frog will show thee the way."

The archer took the jar with the frog, took leave of his mother-in-law and his sisters-in-law, and set out on his way. On he went, and the frog showed him the way. Whether it be far or near, long or short, matters not; suffice it that he came to the fiery river; beyond this river was a high mountain, and on this mountain a door was to be seen. "Kwa, kwa," said the frog, "let me out of the jar, we must cross over this river."

The archer took it out of the jar and placed it on the ground. "Now, my good youth, sit on me. More firmly. Don't be afraid. Thou wilt not smash me."

The youth sat on the frog and pressed it to the very earth. The frog began to swell; it swelled and swelled till it was as large as a haystack. All that the archer now thought of was the risk of falling off.

"If I fall off it will be the death of me," thought he.

The frog, when it had done swelling, took a leap and leaped with one big bound right across the fiery stream, and again made itself quite little.

"Now, good youth, go through that door and I'll wait for thee here; thou wilt come into a cavern, and take care to hide thyself well. In a short time two old men will come; listen to what they are saying, and see what they do, and when they are gone, say and do as they."

The archer went into the mountain, opened the door, and in the cavern it was dark enough to put one's eyes out. He fumbled his way along and felt all about him with his arms till he felt an empty chest, into which he got and hid himself. And now, after he had waited some time, two old men entered and said: "Hi! Shmat-Razum! come and feed us."

At that very instant, there's no telling how, lightning-flashes lit candelabras, in thundered plates and dishes, and various wines and meats appeared upon the table. The old men ate and drank, and then they commanded – "Shmat-Razum! take it all away."

And immediately there was nothing, neither table, nor wine, nor meats, and the candelabras all went out. The archer heard the two old men going out, crept out of the chest, and cried: "Hi!

Shmat-Razum!"

"What is your pleasure?"

"Feed me."

Again everything appeared. The candelabras were lighted, the table was covered, and all the meats and drinks appeared upon it.

The archer sat down at the table and said, "Hi! Shmat-Razum. Come, brother, and sit down with me, let us eat and drink together. I can't stand eating all alone."

And an invisible voice answered him: "Alas! good man, whence hath God sent thee? 'Tis thirty years since I have served right trustily the two old men here, and during all that time they have never once asked me to sit down with them."

The archer looked about him and was amazed. He saw nobody, yet the meats disappeared from the dishes as if someone was sweeping them away, and the wine bottles lifted themselves up, poured themselves into the glasses, and in a trice the glasses were empty. Then the archer went on eating and drinking, but he said: "Hearken, Shmat-Razum! Wilt thou be my servant? Thou shalt have a good time of it with me."

"Why should I not? I have long been growing weary here, and thou, I see, art a good man."

"Well, get everything ready and come with me."

The archer came out of the cave, looked around him, and there was nothing.

"Shmat-Razum, art thou there?"

"I am here. Fear not. I'll never desert thee."

"Right," replied the archer, and he sat him on the frog.

The frog swelled out and leaped across the fiery stream; he placed it in the jar, and set off on his return journey. He came to his mother-in-law and made his new servant regale the old woman and her daughters right royally. Shmat-Razum feasted them so bountifully that the old woman very nearly danced for joy, and ordered the frog three jars of fresh milk every nine days for its faithful services. The archer then took leave of his mother-in-law and wended his way homewards. He went on and on till he was utterly exhausted, his swift feet trembled beneath him, and his white arms sank down by his side.

"Alas!" said he, "Shmat-Razum, dost thou not see how weary I am? My legs fail me."

"Why didst thou not tell it me long ago? I will bring thee to the place alive and well." And immediately the archer was seized by a whirlwind and carried through the air so quickly that his hat fell from his head.

"Hi! Shmat-Razum! Stop a minute. My hat has fallen from my head."

"Too late, master. Thou canst not get it. Thy cap is now 5,000 miles behind thee."

Towns and villages, rivers and forests, melted away beneath the feet of the archer.

And now the archer was flying over the deep sea, and Shmat-Razum said to him: "An thou wilt let me, I would make a golden bower on this sea, and thou wilt be able to rest and be happy!"

"Do so then," said the archer, and straightway they began descending towards the sea. Then, for a moment, the waves splashed high, and then an islet appeared, and on the islet was a golden pleasure-house.

Shmat-Razum said to the archer: "Sit in this pleasure-house and rest and look out upon the sea; three merchant vessels will sail by and stop at the islet. Thou must invite the merchants hither, hospitably entertain them, and exchange me for three wondrous things which the merchants will bring with them. In due time I will return to thee again."

The archer kept watch, and lo! from the west three ships came sailing up, and the merchantmen saw the islet and the golden pleasure-house.

"'Tis a marvel!" said they; "how many times have we not sailed hither, and nothing was to be seen but the sea! and now, behold! a golden pleasure-house is here. Come, friends, let us put to shore and feast our eyes upon it!"

So immediately they lowered the sails and cast the anchor, three of the merchants sat them in a light skiff, and they came to the shore.

"Hail, good man!"

"Hail, ye wayfaring merchants, ye men of many marts! be so good as to turn in to me, stroll about at your ease, make merry and repose; this pleasure-house was built expressly for guests that come by sea!"

The merchants entered the bower and sat them down on footstools.

"Hi! Shmat-Razum!" cried the archer; "give us to eat and drink."

The table appeared, and on the table was wine and savoury meats; whatever the soul desired was there with the wishing. The merchants sighed for envy.

"Come," said they, "let us make an exchange. Thou give us thy servant, and take from us what marvels thou likest best."

"But what marvels have ye then?"

"Look and see!" And one of the merchants drew out of his pocket a little casket, and he had no sooner opened it than a lovely garden spread out all over the island with fragrant flowers and pleasant paths; but when he shut the casket the garden immediately disappeared. The second merchant drew from beneath the folds of his garment an axe, and began to tap with it:

"Rap-tap!" out came a ship.

"Rap-tap!" out came another ship.

A hundred times he rapped, and made a hundred ships with sails and guns and crews complete; the ships sailed, the sailors stood by the guns and took orders from the merchant. The merchant gloried in it for a while, but then he concealed his axe and the ships vanished out of sight just as if they had never been. The third merchant produced a horn, blew into one end of it, and immediately an army appeared, both horse and foot, with cannons and banners, and through all the ranks went the roll of martial music, and the armour of the warriors flashed like fire in the sunlight. The merchant rejoiced in it all, then he took his horn and blew into the other end of it, and there was nothing to be seen, the whole of that martial might was no more.

"Your marvels are well enough, but they are of no use to me," said the archer; "your hosts and your fleets would do honour to a Tsar, but I am only a simple archer. If you would change with me, then must you give me all your three wonders in exchange for my one invisible servant."

"But won't that be too much?"

"Know ye that I'll make no other exchange."

The merchants considered amongst themselves: "What's the use of this garden, these ships, and these hosts to us? 'Twill be better to make the exchange; at any rate we shall always be able to eat and drink our fill without the least trouble."

So they gave the archer their wonders, and said: "Well, Shmat-Razum, we'll take thee with us; wilt thou serve us well and loyally?"

"Why should I not serve you? 'Tis all one with me with whom I live."

The merchants returned to their ships and regaled all their crews right royally.

"Hi! Shmat-Razum! bestir thyself!"

And everyone on board ate and drank his fill and lay down and slept heavily. But the archer sat in his golden bower and grew pensive, and said: "Alas! my heart yearns after my faithful servant, Shmat-Razum. I wonder where he is now!"

"I am here, master!"

The archer was glad. "Is it not time for us to hasten home?"

And he had no sooner spoken than a whirlwind as it were seized him and bore him into the air.

The merchants awoke from their sleep and wanted to drink

away the effects of their carouse.

"Hi! Shmat-Razum, give us some more drink by way of a pick-me-up!"

But no one answered, no one rendered them that service. Order and shout as they might, things remained precisely as they were.

"Well, gentlemen, this sharper has befooled us! The devil take him, and may the island vanish and the golden bower perish." Thus the merchants lamented and lamented, then they spread their sails and departed whither their business called them.

The archer flew back to his country, and descended in a waste place by the blue sea.

"Hi, Shmat-Razum, can we not build us a little castle here?"

"Why not? It shall be ready immediately."

And immediately the castle sprang up, more beautiful than words can tell, 'twas twice as good as a royal palace. The archer opened his casket and a garden immediately appeared round the castle with pleasant country paths and marvellous flowers. There sat the archer at the open window, and quite fell in love with his garden. Suddenly a dove flew in at the window, plumped down upon the ground, and turned into his lovely young wife. They embraced and greeted each other. And the wife said to the archer, "Ever since thou didst leave the house I have been flying as a blue dove among the woods and groves. How happily we will now live together for evermore!"

Early the next morning the King came out on his balcony and looked towards the blue sea, and behold on the very shore stood a new castle, and round the castle was a green garden.

"Who then is this presumptuous stranger who builds on my land without my leave?"

Then his couriers ran thither, asked questions, and came back and told him that this castle was built by the archer, and he himself dwelt in this castle and his wife with him. The King was more angry than ever, and he bade them assemble a host and go to the shores of the sea, root up the garden, smash the castle into little bits, and bring the archer and his wife to him. The archer saw the King's army coming against him, and it was very strong; then he seized his axe quickly and rapped with it, "Rap-tap!"

Out came a ship. He rapped one hundred times, and made one hundred ships. Then he seized his horn and blew once, and a host of footmen rolled out. He blew in the other end, and a host of horse rolled out. The commanders of all the corps came rushing up to him, and asked him for orders. The archer bade them begin the battle. The music struck up, the drums rolled, the regiments moved forwards against the royal host. The infantry, like a solid wall, broke down their centre, the horse cut them off at the wings and took them captive, and the guns from the fleet played upon the capital. The King saw that all his host was flying, rushed forward to stop them – but how? He could not do it, and in a moment he was swept from his horse in the midst of the fierce fight and trampled underfoot. When the fight was over the people assembled together and begged the archer to accept the whole realm from their hands. To this he gave his consent, and ruled that kingdom peaceably all the days of his life.

Some Questions to Reflect Upon:

The archer finds himself in a kingdom where the king and his advisors are deceptive and duplicitous. Have you ever found yourself in a place where those around you could not be trusted?

The archer is the Warrior adventurer figure in this story. He is sent on missions with the intention of his not returning. Have you ever felt like you've been set up?

The archer finds himself on a journey to "Go I know not whither to fetch I know not what." Have you ever risked all on such a journey in your life where you took a great risk not knowing the outcome?

Because of his forthrightness and willing to risk, the archer is made king. He replaces a shadow king and is thus a benevolent and blessing king – a Vibrant Emeritus. Has your lifestyle so far set you up to embrace your inner sovereign?

A Contemporary Story: The Gift of Dialysis

In 2004 I was diagnosed with a kidney disease called IgA Nephropathy, or Berger's Syndrome. I hadn't noticed I was sick. It was discovered by my physician, Rex Lagerstrom, from a routine blood test. Berger's Syndrome is a disease that might be genetic, is likely an autoimmune disease, where the body produces too much protein and the protein destroys the nephrons or filtering system of the kidneys. It is chronic and I have had it since birth. For about 20 percent of patients the disease leads to dialysis. I had had no symptoms. It appeared to come out of the blue.

I began dialysis in the summer of 2007.

For me, life became a time of what the poet TS Eliot called "living and partly living." My body was traumatized three times a week as my blood was filtered by a machine during five-hour dialysis sessions.

I became clinically depressed. Between treatments, I dreamed wild, often terrifying dreams. I woke up screaming on many nights. My brain became cloudy and my ability to do tasks erratic. Various muscles cramped suddenly. I had blood pressure drops, and fainted or nearly fainted when I stood up. My adjustment to temperature changed. Once, my wife Barbara called EMS to our house after I came home from dialysis. I still do not remember their visit.

As my time on dialysis grew and I settled into the treatment lifestyle, I began to wonder what the gift of this disease, this experience, might be. I began to look around the dialysis center at the University of Louisville Kidney Disease Program. Many in the community of the center were African-American. African-

Americans are prone to kidney problems because of tendencies toward high blood pressure and toward diabetes. I began to make a connection with my brothers and sisters in the community of pain. The living and partly living who depended on a machine for life. And I began listening to their hopes and dreams, their stories of faith, and I began listening to my own, to the deep down voice I sometimes connect to if I am still and listen.

Some of those around me chose to be candidates for a transplant. They inspired me. Some others chose not to change their lifestyles to qualify. Still others could not meet the physical qualifications to be candidates. Jim, sitting across from me, had had a transplant when he first was diagnosed but it failed after nineteen days. His brother received a kidney at the same time and was fine after nineteen years. Sometimes, a patient would not come for several days and then his chair was taken by another patient. We were never told when a patient died. They simply disappeared. To qualify one met with a number of doctors from a variety of specialties, a psychiatrist, and a social worker and taking batteries of tests. I qualified six months after I began dialysis. I began praying for the person who would become my donor. I would have to have a cadaverous kidney as my blood type didn't match my wife, children or friends.

I was at a crossroads of my life. I chose life.

I imagined that there was some purpose for me to go through the ordeal of dialysis; and over the three years of my waiting, I included meditation and prayer as part of my five hours of sitting. In my left arm I had a surgically imposed port. The vascular surgeon took a vein and reversed its flow. I could feel the pulse of my blood coursing through my port. (It's called a trill. I can still feel it at the bend of my arm.) It became a pump. Two large needles were inserted there so the blood could exit and reenter my body. I had to hold my arm still throughout the long session. When the session was over, I held pressure at the insertion points until the blood clotted. I still have the trill in my left arm. It reminds me of where I have been and that I may need to return to dialysis if my kidney fails.

One Friday afternoon, in September 2010, a forty year old man took off on a motorcycle and never came home. On Saturday morning my wife and I had driven to Nashville to the Tennessee Arts and Crafts Association annual art show on the grounds of Centennial Park near the Parthenon across from Vanderbilt University. We had been there about ten minutes when the transplant coordinator of the Jewish Hospital in Louisville called and asked me if I were ready for a transplant. The next day, organs from the donor gave new life to six people, two receiving kidneys, one a heart, one lungs, one a liver and one a pancreas.

It is a deep wound and I have a long scar to remind me of life on a razor's edge between life and death.

When I first started dialysis my body jolted to life and I was shocked at how sick I had been without noticing it. With the transplant, I had a similar experience but even more so. Still, recovery was slow. After the first year, having retired, my plan was to write fiction and poetry, grandfather my new grandson and granddaughter, and create a meditation garden in the back yard. I felt quite content. I had fully not chosen life as yet.

Returning to living and to embracing vibrancy and vitality came slowly. During the second spring after my transplant I began to create the meditation garden, by laying the hardscape. This involved carrying creek rock to build walkways, patios, and garden borders. The design work was intuitive rather than highly planned out. I learned to trust feeling and the layout of the garden became a reflection of my inner life, somewhat haphazard but overall meaningful and balanced.

Discussion

There might be no crossroads more intense than that of choosing life over living death. Choosing life can be daunting.

Not everyone who might qualify for a transplant chose to

receive one. Some in the dialysis community chose not to receive a kidney because they feared surgery. Some chose not to because they would have to stop smoking and drinking. Others found it easier to stay on disability. Some allowed their bodies to become so sick they did not qualify and did not want to make the physical changes to receive a kidney.

Each of us comes to this crossroads. We come to a time when we know that without lifestyle changes we will deteriorate more quickly than necessary. We come to a time when we might be bored with all we have done and ask – "Is that all there is?" We might come to believe the culture's disdain, those who are against change, and resign ourselves to staying pat. We might not have the vision to see what a Vibrant Emeritus lifestyle brings to us.

Choosing life is choosing vibrancy. Choosing life is choosing to align our vibrations with those that lead to oneness with the universe, oneness with the abundant, oneness with the unknown.

Challenges

Challenge One: Writing Your Story

1. Reflect on the classic tale *Go I Know Not Whither, to Fetch I Know Not What* and think about its themes, its use of archetypes, and its perspectives on growth, change, and healing.
2. Reflect on the contemporary story and how it connects with the classic tale.
3. Reflect on your own position "at the crossroads," and write your own contemporary story.

Challenge Two: Crossroads Visualization

1. Either read the following visualization into a recorder so that you can play it to yourself or ask a person you trust

to read it to you. Make sure to pause for ten seconds between each line.

2. Place a favorite pen and journal or notebook near to where you are visualizing.

3. Playing soft, meditative music can enhance the experience.

4. Follow the direction of the visualization narrative:

I invite you to lie down on your back in a place where you feel alone,

Just relax and breathe deeply

A deep cleansing breath

Take a deep breath through your nose and

Hold it

And let it go slowly out your mouth

Again

Again

Again

And now as you relax and breathe normally concentrate on the breath as it enters and leaves your nostrils

Just at the place where the breath comes and goes

Until you are completely relaxed

Your neck and shoulders relaxed

Let go of any tension there

Let go

Of any tension in your core, your belly and lower back, just relax

Let go

Of any tension in your hips, your thighs, just relax

Let go

Of any tension in your calves, your knees

Let go

Of any tension in your ankles and feet

Just relax and concentrate on your breath

Coming and going, coming and going
And as you relax imagine that you are out for a walk
There is a path into the woods
The woods are deep
But you take a familiar path
You have been down this path before
And you liked it, it felt good
As you walk, you remember other times
Good memories, treasured insights
You remember when this path was unknown to you
But, over time, you conquered its twists and turns
You feel safe walking, you feel connected
And you go further and further, deeper and deeper,
Until you get to the place in the road that is the farthest you've
      been
But you are feeling good, and you feel intrigued about what's
      beyond
So you move further, deeper, into the woods,
Away from the way you know
Further and further in
Until you come to a crossroads
The road you've taken is well worn
And it continues on further and further
Many footsteps have worn down this way
But there is something about the other path,
Not so traveled, not so worn
But taken by some because there is a path
And it moves in a new direction
So you sit in the center of the two roads
Looking back from where you came gives you joy
Gives you good feelings, gives you pride in your journey
But the other path looks inviting, too
Both paths have twists and turns
And take you to you know not where

The path you came on seems like a good way to go
To continue to feel what you have always felt
But there is also something about the other path
What's down that path? Where does it lead?
Not many choose it, but maybe it's for you.
How will you choose?
How will you choose?
How will you choose?
So begin to come back into the room
Slowly,
Slowly
Sit up slowly,
And find your favorite pen and notebook or journal
Begin to write about the advantages of choosing each of the
   ways.

Challenge Three: Angeles Arrien's Five Signs of Life

The cultural anthropologist Angeles Arrien wrote a book based on her examination of the symbols used by all the known cultures in the world. According to her research, five of these symbols appear in every culture: the square, the circle, the triangle, the spiral and the equidistant cross. Each of the symbols has a meaning:

Square: Solidity, strong base, concern with the basics – home, finances, physical comfort, food and shelter.

Circle: Completeness, wholeness, a balance of the physical, mental, emotional, and spiritual. Having come to a place where one feels whole.

Triangle: Visionary, seeing possible destinations for our lives, new possibilities.

Spiral: The journey, a willingness to take risks, the lure of newness, movement toward a goal even when one does not know how one might get there.

Equidistant Cross: Relationship, our primary relationship with a mate or Lover, our relationship to ourselves, our relationship to community, our relationship to a higher consciousness.

1. Using Arrien's book, *Signs of Life*, follow the directions there for randomly selecting a sequence of the symbols.
2. Using Arrien's book, examine the meaning of the sequence:

A focus that is coming up in your life
What you are presently skilled at doing
The central focus you are concerned with now
A focus that you have completed that allows you to be focused where you are now
An issue you are so complete with, it's over; or, you are in denial and don't want to look at it

Challenge Four: What Option Will I Take?

1. It is useful to use a legal style pad to do this activity.
2. Using a ruler or straight edge, divide the page vertically.
3. Label the left-hand column: "Staying in My Warrior" and label the right-hand column "Stepping into My Elder."
4. List all the advantages you now have as a Warrior on the left side. On the right-hand side, list all the advantages you might receive if you are willing to step into your Elder status.
5. As you examine each column, make a list of the obstacles that come up for you that prevent you from moving into the Vibrant Emeritus energy.

A Poem to Contemplate

The Road Not Taken
By Robert Frost

Two roads diverged in a yellow wood,
And sorry I could not travel both
And be one traveler, long I stood
And looked down one as far as I could
To where it bent in the undergrowth;

Then took the other, as just as fair,
And having perhaps the better claim
Because it was grassy and wanted wear,
Though as for that the passing there
Had worn them really about the same,

And both that morning equally lay
In leaves no step had trodden black.
Oh, I marked the first for another day!
Yet knowing how way leads on to way
I doubted if I should ever come back.

I shall be telling this with a sigh
Somewhere ages and ages hence:
Two roads diverged in a wood, and I,
I took the one less traveled by,
And that has made all the difference.

Some Questions to Reflect Upon:

In this culture, many men fear taking the path of the Elder and this is often the road less traveled. What difference might taking the path of the Elder make?

At other crossroads, have you taken the more traveled or less traveled road? What difference did your choice make?

Do you ever look back and regret your choices?

Do you ever take a path and not look back?

How do you know that you have chosen the best path for you?

Practice

Use the procedure Angeles Arrien outlined in her book *Signs of Life* at key times such as once a month, on New Year's Day, on one's birthday, whenever one reaches a critical period in one's life.

Keep a log and see how your life progresses from one concern to another, from crossroads to crossroads.

Growth Questions

As a man living in a culture that worships youth, dishonors Elders, and embraces competition without integrity, am I ready to create a second half of life that benefits others, mentors and teaches those who will come after me, and is spiritually based?

How difficult is it for me to let go of what has been and "go I know not whither to bring back I know not what?"

Do I find myself at a crossroads as a mature man not knowing what my next life journey might be?

What fears about aging do I currently hold?

How might I overcome these fears?

What life changes did I make earlier in my life when I was at a crossroads? Was I successful? What did I learn then that might help now as I consider new risks?

Chapter 5

Becoming Generative

*I come to a clearing. I sit upon the ground and look deeply into the sky.
I remember looking up at the sky as a youth. I had such dreams! I was
inspired! Can I return to those golden dreams? Can I make them real
with what I now know?*
This is the fourth task.

Elders are the jewels of humanity that have been mined from
the Earth, cut in the rough, then buffed and polished by the
stonecutter's art into precious gems that we recognize for their
enduring value and beauty. Shaped with patience and love
over decades of refinement, each facet of the jewel reflects
light that awakens our soul to intimations of its own splendor.
We sense such radiance in our youth, but we cannot contain it.
It requires a lifetime's effort to carve out the multifaceted
structure that can display our hidden splendor in all its glory.
– Zalman Schachter-Shalomi and Ronald S. Miller, *From Age-
ing to Sage-ing*

The Task: Becoming Generative by Merging Innocence with Sagacity

Author Drew Leder, in his book *Spiritual Passages*, writes:

Erikson felt that much of life is preparing for the middle
adulthood stage and the last stage is recovering from it.
Perhaps that is because as older adults we can often look back
on our lives with happiness and are content, feeling fulfilled
with a deep sense that life has meaning and we've made a
contribution to life, a feeling Erikson calls integrity. Our
strength comes from a wisdom that the world is very large

and we now have a detached concern for the whole of life, accepting death as the completion of life.

On the other hand, some adults may reach this stage and despair at their experiences and perceived failures. They may fear death as they struggle to find a purpose to their lives, wondering "Was the trip worth it?" Alternatively, they may feel they have all the answers (not unlike going back to adolescence) and end with a strong dogmatism that only their view has been correct.

The significant relationship is with all of mankind — "my-kind."

It is the task of the Vibrant Emeritus to find this stage of what Erikson calls integrity. Jungian psychologist Allan Chinen suggests that this can be achieved making a connection to the idealism of the "Golden Child" and merging it with the self-transcended mature adult. The task is a task of sorting to the positive concerning the meaning of one's life, keeping alive the idealism of one's youth and merging it with the wisdom and practical knowledge one has gained by living.

In the Legend of Parsifal, Parsifal lived an idyllic childhood deep in the forest. The forest in stories is often a symbol of the unconscious. It is a place where, as one ages, the Golden Child (our original creative, abundant and limitless child) lives. Parsifal's mother, Heart's Sorrow, has taken great pains to raise her son here away from the real life (consciousness) and its challenges. Parsifal is raised in both ignorance of the "real life" of adults and innocence. When he sees the five knights, his desire to leave childhood and become an adult is stirred. Later, having lived his life as the greatest knight in the world, he rests with the Fisher King and enters again the Grail Castle, combining his Golden Child with his Elder Wisdom.

Deep within us is the "Golden Child" whose innocence and creativity knows no bounds. By using this wild energy, one can free oneself from social conventions, the generally held beliefs that bind us and limit what we might become if we liberate ourselves. The Vibrant Emeritus who, having transcended the norms, confines and consciousness of one's Warrior years, is now free to dream again the dreams one dreamed as a youth, live according to the noble virtues imagined as a youth, and create the world within his own kingly realm that one has long envisioned. It is a kingdom that expands and a vision that looks outward rather than the ego-centered middle years. In so doing the Vibrant Emeritus heals and blesses oneself, those one loves and those who enter his realm.

Having made the decision to move forward, we discover that within us might be found the direction we have been looking for: our youthful inspirations, our better selves. I have worked with many populations including men in prison to men attending the New Warrior Training Adventure, to military veterans, to men in recovery from addictions. Even in the most desperate of situations, including a man on death row, I have never met a man who as a youth did not have noble and inspiring dreams for oneself, one's family, and who still didn't believe in one's most deeply held hopes and aspirations.

At the beginning of Parsifal's Quest, he sees the five knights who he takes as angels or demigods. These figures represent those glorious and noble visions we have as a youth. Parsifal is at the edge of puberty and will meet the stirrings of his male heart when he meets the woman in the tent he takes for a cathedral. Filled with youthful passion, his hubris high and his blood running hot, he challenges and defeats the Red Knight and takes on his armor: the armor of the Warrior. When his adventures end and he lets go of this mask taking off the armor, he enters the Grail Castle of deep spirituality and transformation. It is here that he can merge the shining noble visions the five knights first presented to him with his hard-won wisdom, and transcend the Warrior life. Now he enters the place where noble youth and maidens present him with the symbols of the Christian faith (emblems of his spirituality).

The Vibrant Emeritus is a man who moves one's vision from personal reward to those youthful and ennobling aspirations that one may now have the strength, patience, and wisdom as the guiding force of life.

Many men have a difficult time letting go of ego-driven pursuits and rewards. But what becomes possible for the Vibrant Emeritus is personal transcendence and rewards that are not temporal, temporary, finite or competitive. They are deeply felt and speak to one's deepest aspirations for oneself including those of blessing, abundance of character, and mentoring from the deepest possible wisdom. It is a life built on listening, responding, giving, teaching, and supporting without attachment to one's own desires, with a specific outcome in mind, inspiring quietly and thoughtfully, and allowing the mentee his own independent growth, selection of outcomes and discovery of practice and way.

Transcending the self, the ego, is necessary for the Vibrant Emeritus to free himself, to be joyful and free. One on this path of letting go keeps his shadows conscious, honors but releases one's Warrior achievement, and makes a firm decision to take the path of personal commitment and authenticity: the first three tasks of the Vibrant Emeritus.

The lure of personal glory and staying in one place can be very comfortable. But this comfort can lead one to shadow mentoring (it feels so good to be the Guide to the mentee), shadow spirituality (I'm okay with where I am, no need to go deeper), and shadow authenticity.

I have met Elders who were aging not "sage-ing," sitting and pontificating rather than standing in their power, offering judgments and advice when it wasn't asked for, became in love with their voice, refused to give space to mentees, and spent their time reminiscing and storytelling to no purpose. Each of these men, sadly, were stuck in tradition, the guise of what looked like Eldering, wearing the masks they hadn't loosened and left as they moved forward. They became the stuck and manipulating older brothers in *The Water of Life* story, and not the wise mentor.

Generativity is a concept of psychologist Erik Erikson and has been defined as the following:

> One of the key features of midlife is the opportunity to pass along the wisdom of our accumulated years onto others. Psychologist Erik Erikson used the term "generativity" to capture the need for all of us to leave something behind for future generations. The opposite of generativity is "stagnation" in which you throw your energy not into helping others, but into focusing on yourself and your personal needs. Generativity has the benefit of helping your personality flourish, even while you provide vital sustenance and support to the next generation. Stagnation carries the risk that all of your growth potential turns inward, and ultimately disappears altogether.
> – Susan Krauss Whitbourne, "The Joys of Generativity in Midlife,"*Huffington Post*, 2/06/2013

The Vibrant Emeritus embodies these concepts in all his relationships and it becomes the focus of his activities in this stage of life.

A Classic Tale

Wali Dad, the Simple Grass Cutter

(A. Lang, *The Brown Fairy Book*)

Once upon a time there lived a poor old man whose name was Wali Dad Gunjay, or Wali Dad the Bald. He had no relations, but lived all by himself in a little mud hut some distance from any town, and made his living by cutting grass in the jungle, and selling it as fodder for horses. He only earned by this five halfpence a day; but he was a simple old man, and needed so little out of it, that he saved up one halfpenny daily, and spent the rest upon such food and clothing as he required.

In this way he lived for many years until, one night, he thought that he would count the money he had hidden away in the great earthen pot under the floor of his hut. So he set to work, and with much trouble he pulled the bag out on to the floor, and sat gazing in astonishment at the heap of coins which tumbled out of it. What should he do with them all? he wondered. But he never thought of spending the money on himself, because he was content to pass the rest of his days as he had been doing for ever so long, and he really had no desire for any greater comfort or luxury.

At last he threw all the money into an old sack, which he pushed under his bed, and then, rolled in his ragged old blanket, he went off to sleep.

Early next morning he staggered off with his sack of money to the shop of a jeweller, whom he knew in the town, and bargained with him for a beautiful little gold bracelet. With this carefully wrapped up in his cotton waistband he went to the house of a rich friend, who was a travelling merchant, and used to wander about with his camels and merchandise through many countries. Wali Dad was lucky enough to find him at home, so he sat down, and after a little talk he asked the merchant who was the most virtuous and beautiful lady he had ever met with. The merchant replied that the princess of Khaistan was renowned everywhere as well for the beauty of her person as for the kindness and generosity of her disposition.

"Then," said Wali Dad, "next time you go that way, give her this little bracelet, with the respectful compliments of one who admires virtue far more than he desires wealth."

With that he pulled the bracelet from his waistband, and handed it to his friend. The merchant was naturally much astonished, but said nothing, and made no objection to carrying out his friend's plan.

Time passed by, and at length the merchant arrived in the course of his travels at the capital of Khaistan. As soon as he had an opportunity he presented himself at the palace, and sent in the bracelet, neatly packed in a little perfumed box provided by himself, giving at the same time the message entrusted to him by Wali Dad.

The princess could not think who could have bestowed this present on her, but she bade her servant to tell the merchant that if he would return, after he had finished his business in the city, she would give him her reply. In a few days, therefore, the merchant came back, and received from the princess a return present in the shape of a camel-load of rich silks, besides a present of money for himself. With these he set out on his journey.

Some months later he got home again from his journeyings, and proceeded to take Wali Dad the princess' present. Great was the perplexity of the good man to find a camel-load of silks tumbled at his door! What was he to do with these costly things? But, presently, after much thought, he begged the merchant to consider whether he did not know of some young prince to whom such treasures might be useful.

"Of course," cried the merchant, greatly amused; "from Delhi to Baghdad, and from Constantinople to Lucknow, I know them all; and there lives none worthier than the gallant and wealthy young prince of Nekabad."

"Very well, then, take the silks to him, with the blessing of an old man," said Wali Dad, much relieved to be rid of them.

So, the next time that the merchant journeyed that way he carried the silks with him, and in due course arrived at Nekabad, and sought an audience of the prince. When he was shown into his presence he produced the beautiful gift of silks that Wali Dad had sent, and begged the young man to accept them as a humble tribute to his worth and greatness. The prince was much touched by the generosity of the giver, and ordered, as a return present, twelve of the finest breed of horses for which his country was famous to be delivered over to the merchant, to whom also, before he took his leave, he gave a munificent reward for his services.

As before, the merchant at last arrived at home; and next day, he set out for Wali Dad's house with the twelve horses. When the old man saw them coming in the distance he said to himself: "Here's luck! a troop of horses coming! They are sure to want quantities of grass, and I shall sell all I have without having to drag it to market." Thereupon he rushed off and cut grass as fast he could. When he got back, with as much grass as he could possibly carry, he was greatly discomfited to find that the horses were all for himself. At first he could not think what to do with them, but, after a little while, a brilliant idea struck him! He gave two to the merchant, and begged him to take the rest to the princess of Khaistan, who was clearly the fittest person to possess such beautiful animals.

The merchant departed, laughing. But, true to his old friend's request, he took the horses with him on his next journey, and eventually presented them safely to the princess. This time the princess sent for the merchant, and questioned him about the giver. Now, the merchant was usually a most honest man, but he did not quite like to describe Wali Dad in his true light as an old man whose income was five halfpence a day, and who had hardly clothes to cover him. So he told her that his friend had heard stories of her beauty and goodness, and had longed to lay the best he had at her feet. The princess then took her father into her confidence, and begged him to advise her what courtesy she might return to one who persisted in making her such presents.

"Well," said the king, "you cannot refuse them; so the best thing you can do is to send this friend at once a present so magnificent that he is not likely to be able to send you anything better, and so will be ashamed to send anything at all!" Then he ordered that, in place of each of the ten horses, two mules laden with silver should be returned by her.

Thus, in a few hours, the merchant found himself in charge of a splendid caravan; and he had to hire a number of armed men to defend it on the road against the robbers, and he was glad indeed to find himself back again in Wali Dad's hut.

"Well, now," cried Wali Dad, as he viewed all the wealth laid at his door, "I can well repay that kind prince for his magnificent present of horses; but to be sure you have been put to great expenses! Still, if you will accept six mules and their loads, and will take the rest straight to Nekabad, I shall thank you heartily."

The merchant felt handsomely repaid for his trouble, and wondered greatly how the matter would turn out. So he made no difficulty about it; and as soon as he could get things ready, he set out for Nekabad with this new and princely gift.

This time the prince, too, was embarrassed, and questioned the merchant closely. The merchant felt that his credit was at stake, and whilst inwardly determining that he would not carry the joke any further, could not help describing Wali Dad in such glowing terms that the old man would never have known himself had he heard them. The prince, like the king of Khaistan, determined that he would send in return a gift that would be truly royal, and which would perhaps prevent the giver sending him anything more. So he made up a caravan on twenty splendid horses caparisoned in gold embroidered cloths, with fine Moroccan saddles and silver bridles and stirrups, also twenty camels of the best breed, which had the speed of racehorses, and could swing along at a trot all day without getting tired; and, lastly, twenty elephants, with magnificent silver howdahs and coverings of silk embroidered with pearls. To take care of these animals the merchant hired a little army of men; and the troop made a great show as they traveled along.

When Wali Dad from a distance saw the cloud of dust which the caravan made, and the glitter of its appointments, he said to himself: "By Allah! here's a grand crowd coming! Elephants, too! Grass will be selling well to-day!" And with that he hurried off to the jungle and cut grass as fast as he could. As soon as he got back he found the caravan had stopped at his door, and the merchant was waiting, a little anxiously, to tell him the news and to congratulate him upon his riches.

"Riches!" cried Wali Dad, "what has an old man like me with one foot in the grave to do with riches? That beautiful young princess, now! She'd be the one to enjoy all these fine things! Do you take for yourself two horses, two camels, and two elephants, with all their trappings, and present the rest to her."

The merchant at first objected to these remarks, and pointed out to Wali Dad that he was beginning to feel these embassies a little awkward. Of course he was himself richly repaid, so far as expenses went; but still he did not like going so often, and he was getting nervous. At length, however, he consented to go once more, but he promised himself never to embark on another such enterprise.

So, after a few days' rest, the caravan started off once more for Khaistan.

The moment the king of Khaistan saw the gorgeous train of men and beasts entering his palace courtyard, he was so amazed that he hurried down in person to inquire about it, and became dumb when he heard that these also were a present from the princely Wali Dad, and were for the princess, his daughter. He went hastily off to her apartments, and said to her: "I tell you what it is, my dear, this man wants to marry you; that is the meaning of all these presents! There is nothing for it but that we go and pay him a visit in person. He must be a man of immense wealth, and as he is so devoted to you, perhaps you might do worse than marry him!"

The princess agreed with all that her father said, and orders were issued for vast numbers of elephants and camels, and gorgeous tents and flags, and litters for the ladies, and horses for the men, to be prepared without delay, as the king and princess were going to pay a visit to the great and munificent prince Wali Dad. The merchant, the king declared, was to guide the party.

The feelings of the poor merchant in this sore dilemma can hardly be imagined. Willingly would he have run away; but he was treated with so much hospitality as Wali Dad's representative, that he hardly got an instant's real peace, and never any opportunity of slipping away. In fact, after a few days, despair possessed him to such a degree that he made up his mind that all that happened was fate, and that escape was impossible; but he hoped devoutly some turn of fortune would reveal to him a way out of the difficulties which he had, with the best intentions, drawn upon himself.

On the seventh day they all started, amidst thunderous salutes from the ramparts of the city, and much dust, and cheering, and blaring of trumpets.

Day after day they moved on, and every day the poor merchant felt more ill and miserable. He wondered what kind of death the king would invent for him, and went through almost as much torture, as he lay awake nearly the whole of every night thinking over the situation, as he would have suffered if the king's executioners were already setting to work upon his neck.

At last they were only one day's march from Wali Dad's little mud home. Here a great encampment was made, and the merchant was sent on to tell Wali Dad that the King and Princess of Khaistan had arrived and were seeking an interview. When the merchant arrived he found the poor old man eating his evening meal of onions and dry bread, and when he told him of all that had happened he had not the heart to proceed to load him with the reproaches which rose to his tongue. For Wali Dad was overwhelmed with grief and shame for himself, for his friend, and for the name and honour of the princess; and he wept and plucked at his beard, and groaned most piteously. With tears he begged the merchant to detain them for one day by any kind of excuse he could think of, and to come in the morning to discuss what they should do.

As soon as the merchant was gone Wali Dad made up his mind that there was only one honourable way out of the shame and distress that he had created by his foolishness, and that was – to kill himself. So, without stopping to ask anyone's advice, he went off in the middle of the night to a place where the river wound along at the base of steep rocky cliffs of great height, and determined to throw himself down and put an end to his life. When he got to the place he drew back a few paces, took a little run, and at the very edge of that dreadful black gulf he stopped short! He COULD not do it!

From below, unseen in the blackness of the deep night shadows, the water roared and boiled round the jagged rocks – he could picture the place as he knew it, only ten times more pitiless and forbidding in the visionless darkness; the wind soughed through the gorge with fearsome sighs, and rustlings and whisperings, and the bushes and grasses that grew in the ledges of the cliffs seemed to him like living creatures that danced and beckoned, shadowy and indistinct. An owl laughed "Hoo! hoo!" almost in his face, as he peered over the edge of the gulf, and the old man threw himself back in a perspiration of horror. He was afraid! He drew back shuddering, and covering his face in his hands he wept aloud.

Presently he was aware of a gentle radiance that shed itself before him. Surely morning was not already coming to hasten and reveal his disgrace! He took his hands from before his face, and saw before him two lovely beings whom his instinct told him were not mortal, but were Peris from Paradise.

"Why do you weep, old man?" said one, in a voice as clear and musical as that of the bulbul.

"I weep for shame," replied he.

"What do you do here?" questioned the other.

"I came here to die," said Wali Dad. And as they questioned

him, he confessed all his story.

Then the first stepped forward and laid a hand upon his shoulder, and Wali Dad began to feel that something strange – what, he did not know – was happening to him. His old cotton rags of clothes were changed to beautiful linen and embroidered cloth; on his hard, bare feet were warm, soft shoes, and on his head a great jewelled turban. Round his neck there lay a heavy golden chain, and the little old bent sickle, which he cut grass with, and which hung in his waistband, had turned into a gorgeous scimitar, whose ivory hilt gleamed in the pale light like snow in moonlight. As he stood wondering, like a man in a dream, the other peri waved her hand and bade him turn and see; and, lo! before him a noble gateway stood open. And up an avenue of giant plane trees the peris led him, dumb with amazement. At the end of the avenue, on the very spot where his hut had stood, a gorgeous palace appeared, ablaze with myriads of lights. Its great porticoes and verandahs were occupied by hurrying servants, and guards paced to and fro and saluted him respectfully as he drew near, along mossy walks and through sweeping grassy lawns where fountains were playing and flowers scented the air. Wali Dad stood stunned and helpless.

"Fear not," said one of the peris; "go to your house, and learn that God rewards the simple-hearted."

With these words they both disappeared and left him. He walked on, thinking still that he must be dreaming. Very soon he retired to rest in a splendid room, far grander than anything he had ever dreamed of.

When morning dawned he woke, and found that the palace, and himself, and his servants were all real, and that he was not dreaming after all!

If he was dumbfounded, the merchant, who was ushered into his presence soon after sunrise, was much more so. He told Wali Dad that he had not slept all night, and by the first streak of daylight had started to seek out his friend. And what a search he had had! A great stretch of wild jungle country had, in the night, been changed into parks and gardens; and if it had not been for some of Wali Dad's new servants, who found him and brought him to the palace, he would have fled away under the impression that his trouble had sent him crazy, and that all he saw was only imagination.

Then Wali Dad told the merchant all that had happened. By his advice he sent an invitation to the king and princess of Khaistan to come and be his guests, together with all their retinue and servants, down to the very humblest in the camp.

For three nights and days a great feast was held in honour of the royal guests. Every evening the king and his nobles were served on golden plates and from golden cups; and the smaller people on silver plates and from silver cups; and each evening each guest was requested to keep the plates and cups that they had used as a remembrance of the occasion. Never had anything so splendid been seen. Besides the great dinners, there were sports and hunting, and dances, and amusements of all sorts.

On the fourth day the king of Khaistan took his host aside, and asked him whether it was true, as he had suspected, that he wished to marry his daughter. But Wali Dad, after thanking him very much for the compliment, said that he had never dreamed of so great an honour, and that he was far too old and ugly for so fair a lady; but he begged the king to stay with him until he could send for the Prince of Nekabad, who was a most excellent, brave, and honourable young man, and would surely be delighted to try to win the hand of the beautiful princess.

To this the king agreed, and Wali Dad sent the merchant to Nekabad, with a number of attendants, and with such handsome presents that the prince came at once, fell head over ears in love with the princess, and married her at Wali Dad's palace amidst a fresh outburst of rejoicings.

And now the King of Khaistan and the Prince and Princess of Nekabad each went back to their own country; and Wali Dad lived to a good old age, befriending all who were in trouble and preserving, in his prosperity, the simple-hearted and generous nature that he had when he was only Wali Dad Gunjay, the grass cutter.

Some Questions to Reflect Upon:

The humble grass cutter has reached a time in his life where he assesses what he has earned during his working life and decides to refocus by purchasing a bracelet and sending it to an ideal of beauty and virtue embodied by the Princess of the East. Clearly his change of direction in his life is to look outward from himself toward youthful and noble ideals. What ideals might you revisit as you move from egocentric focus to a focus on your generativity?

The old man's simple gift leads to greater and greater abundancy. His generativity creates greater wealth for all involved. At no time in the story does he consider keeping this wealth for himself and ultimately he creates unity in the marriage of the prince and princess, uniting the land. What noble acts might you be able to generate within your family and community?

The gift the old man originally gives causes major changes in the land. What small gift might you give?

A Contemporary Story

I was born in 1948, a baby boomer, and grew up in the relative security of a German immigrant neighborhood: Snitzelburg, in the heart of Germantown, near downtown Louisville, Kentucky. Our Catholic parish was Saint Elizabeth of Hungary. There were only two Protestant families who lived near the street where I lived. Dwight Eisenhower was president. Few people thought about moving to the suburbs. Mothers were homemakers, and knew and looked out for all the kids on the block.

Because I was Catholic, the 1960 election between Kennedy and Nixon was especially important. The pastor of our church was a known Democrat who was often asked to open sessions of the Kentucky Legislature with a prayer. Bert Combs was elected governor from the liberal wing of the Democratic Party and was an early supporter of Kennedy. It was exciting for us to think that a Catholic might be president, a young man who promised change. The teaching nuns at our school kept us well informed of the Kennedy campaign and election. In classroom voting, only one of us voted for Nixon.

When Kennedy won I was elated. A copy of his Inaugural Address hung in our classroom and we studied it with fervor. When he established the Peace Corps, we did projects on countries where we might want to serve. My heart began to believe that I could make a positive difference in the world. I believed it so thoroughly that for most of my life I have taken jobs that promised to promote personal and communal change: as a middle school teacher at an experimental school; as director of a drug and alcohol treatment center for youth and adults; as a master trainer implementing Student Assistance Programs and promoting youth resiliency; and as an author for the Research Press.

Another source of youthful ideals and noble ambitions came from the Prayer of Saint Francis: *Make Me an Instrument of Your Peace.* I am not sure which nun in grade school or brother in high school introduced me to this prayer. When I read it for the first time, it touched me deeply and became a kind of mission statement for my life.

I have been lucky in my life to do work that I love because it was work that promoted personal change in me and in those with whom I was honored to work.

When I turned 50, much of that changed. After the 9/11 attacks, funding for the positive youth development work I was doing dried up and the training program I worked for closed its doors. Soon after, I was diagnosed with end-stage renal failure. I thought my career had come to an end. The kidney transplant I received in 2010 renewed my life.

At the age of 62, still in recovery and with weak energy, I was listed as disabled. It took almost three years to regain my energy to the point where I could staff New Warrior Training Adventures, renew my journey to be certified as a Ritual Elder in the Warrior Community, do occasional trainings for school staffs and adolescents, and turn my attention to what being an Elder meant.

A year ago, in 2012, I suddenly got a great burst of energy. I spent the summer making stone patios, tilling beds, selecting and planting perennials, and making walkways in what would be my meditation and writing garden. I called my friend Jon with whom I had traveled and we planned to restart the writing careers we had planned as young men. He was taking a master's degree in creative writing at City College. The garden was part of my plan to live a writer's life, returning to writing novels and poetry again after forty years. I would plant my garden, write for several hours a day, produce a line of detective novels and enter poetry contests. I won a prize with my first attempt that year.

I soon discovered that making the garden *was* my meditation, and that the energy and physical strength it took to make it invigorated me and sent me in a totally different direction. I began talking with my Elder mentor, Alan Podbelsek, about taking part again on the Mankind Project's New Warrior Training Adventure (MKP/NWTA). I started by joining the Men of Service team for a part of one weekend, then the full weekend on the next NWTA. In our conversations over coffee and lunch, I began to talk quite casually about the concept that maybe at the close of our working years there ought to be a rite of passage as meaningful and experiential as the NWTA. It was just an idea. I was just floating the concept as it came up, dreamlike, in my consciousness. I had no plans for developing a weekend initiation experience. Just talk.

The deeper I delved into being an Elder in the Kentucky MKP community and in my life, the more it seemed right, physically, emotionally, mentally and spiritually. When I had turned fifty, I was asked by two leaders to perform the leading Elder role on an NWTA weekend. I declared in a simple ceremony at a community meeting that I wanted to be seen as an Elder. I began the newly formed process MKP had designed for men doing this role on the NWTA weekend. It was an abortive attempt in a way, in that I fulfilled all the requirements except two when I discovered I had end-stage kidney failure.

I was not ready, though I believed I was. I held in me the arrogance of one who could portray a role but not the life experience to, in a deeply spiritual way, perform it.

In my life, all the meaningful elements (family, relationships, career) have been unplanned by me but in some way I have been guided. That is, I was fortunate to be open enough to accept opportunities that seemed to appear. When I accepted the opportunity that felt right and meant for me, doors opened, I met the right mentors, choices became easier. When I have attempted to force my life in some sort of logical progression, nothing works out. But when I meet the right person and set of circumstances, off I go on a new and significant adventure. I have not looked for a job since I answered an ad for a teaching position at the Saint Francis School in 1974.

This past year I announced to my friends, family, and MKP community my desire to resume on a partial basis my career as a professional trainer, facilitator and coach. Within twenty-four hours I had two outstanding partners who wanted to put together a consortium offering training to executives in the area of leadership development, training and coaching. My friend, Stephen McCrocklin, president of the Langsford Center, asked me to do a two-hour presentation to a group of special needs coordinators and school counselors. I found myself hired to facilitate one youth and two adult retreats. My partners in our new consortium have found several opportunities for us to begin our work with companies and individuals.

The quiet voice that had been insisting on my looking at initiation for Elders became overwhelming last January. I did a web search for Elder initiation in traditional societies, Jungian archetypes for Elders, and authors and other sources who might be working in the area. I was deluged by energy for this project and very quickly I discovered the sources I would find most useful for putting together a weekend experience, and later a center on Elder initiation. The three most powerful sources were Allan Chinen, John C. Robinson, and Angeles Arrien. Chinen, whose series of books on Elder tales, Jungian interpretation and his delineation of the seven tasks of an Elder form the skeleton of the Vibrant Emeritus Initiation Experience. John C. Robinson recently published *What Aging Men Want: The Odyssey as a Parable of Male Aging* and his interpretation of the Odysseus myth informs this work. For many years, I had read and used the materials developed by cultural anthropologist Angeles Arrien. I was delighted to discover her book and tape course: *The Second Half of Life: Opening the Eight Gates of Wisdom.*

As I was developing this book, I discovered that my friend and colleague Michael Gurian was publishing *The Wonder of Aging: A New Approach to Embracing Life After Fifty.* When I was a program developer for National Training Associates, I read and became very excited by Michael's books on youth: *The Wonder of Boys, The Wonder of Girls, A Fine Young Man* and *Boys and Girls Learn Differently.* His work became the underlying research and thought for my trainings and books on positive youth development. This most recent book and our conversations regarding the wonder of aging provide the underpinnings for both this book and the work of the Vibrant Emeritus Center, a center devoted to providing outstanding training to men and women entering the last third of their lives.

Quickly, I had a title for the project: "Vibrant Emeritus."

"Vibrant" comes from the ideas of an MKP Elder Augustin Gurule, who talks about the idea that everything is vibration including our bodies and everything we see that appears solid and our relationships with each other, with God and with ourselves. "Emeritus" from the idea of emeritus status given to men and women who have completed their careers but are still offering guidance and mentorship to younger men and women on college campuses, in corporations, and in other areas.

Ideas and concepts flowed like rain into a rain barrow after a spring thunderstorm. I completed a training manual in a few months. I searched out other Elders who might be interested. I sent my manuscript to men I considered role models and who appeared to be embracing their Elder and emeritus years with grace, wisdom and positivity. Master trainer Tim Schladand wrote back with enthusiasm and spirit, and we sustain each other in developing this process. Together, we put together an inaugural Vibrant Emeritus Initiation in December 2013.

My work now on consciously embracing my Elder years as a time of providing abundance, blessing and mentoring to others and to support the work of other Elders in doing the same rests again on those noble ideas of my youth, on the energetic young president and his challenges to my generation and to the eternal challenge provided in the simple prayer of Saint Francis. I am no longer engaged in earning or collecting new achievements or building family. My energy is reserved for moving toward letting go of ego concerns and fulfilling the old verities taught to me in my youth.

Discussion

These are stories about generativity and the abundance that flows from it. Erik Erikson uses the term "generativity" for men in the second half of life who let go of their egocentricity and move their conscious behavior towards generating blessing, wisdom, giving, listening, grace, and abundance for the good of others.

In the story of the "Simple Grass Cutter", the Elder at the center of the story has accumulated a small treasure from the work for which he has labored. It is time for him to take an account and no longer store up what he has earned and achieved. He has come to a crossroads in his life and has decided to move to a new consciousness and a new direction. He is no longer toiling to build up wealth. In fact, he decides that he wants to live as he has as a simple grass cutter. The first instinct of this "goodly man" is to give the money to a princess who is not only beautiful but virtuous. Immediately, this act generates more wealth which is then given to a handsome, virtuous young man: the prince.

More and more abundance grows and over and over the grass cutter gives it away. At last, because of the generativity of the old man's initial gift, the prince and princess marry, uniting the land from east to west. Although honored and bestowed with a house, the grass cutter returns to his simple life, wiser and more generative having renewed the community and the kingdom.

Challenge One: Writing Your Story

1. Reflect on the classic tale of the "Simple Grass Cutter" and think about its themes, its use of archetypes, and its perspectives on growth, change, and healing.
2. Reflect on the contemporary story and how it connects with the classic tale.
3. Reflect on your own youthful values, goals and dreams, and your Elder sagacity. Write your own contemporary story.

Challenge Two: The Vision of Youth/the Sagacity of the Elder

1. Either read the following visualization into a recorder so that you can play it to yourself or ask a person you trust

to read it to you. Make sure to pause for ten seconds between each line.

2. Place a favorite pen and notebook or journal near to the place where you are visualizing.

3. Playing soft, meditative music can enhance the experience.

4. Follow the direction of the visualization narrative:

I invite you to lie down on your back in a place where you feel alone,
Just relax and breathe deeply
A deep cleansing breath
Take a deep breath through your nose and
Hold it
Hold it
And let it go slowly out your mouth
(Do this 3 more times)
And now as you relax and breathe normally concentrate on the breath as it enters and leaves your nostrils
Just at the place where the breath comes and goes
Until you are completely relaxed
Your neck and shoulders relaxed
Let go of any tension there
Let go
Of any tension in your core, your belly and lower back, just relax
Let go
Of any tension in your hips, your thighs, just relax
Let go
Of any tension in your calves, your knees
Let go
Of any tension in your ankles and feet
Just relax and concentrate on your breath
Coming and going, coming and going

And as you relax imagine that you are out for a walk
It is a beautiful day; the sun is warm but not hot
The breezes touch your face, it is an easy walk
You come to a wood
You can see the sun shining in the woods
You do not hesitate to enter, but find a way into the woods
There are trees and plants and bushes all around
There is a path and you find it
And walking down the path you listen to the forest sounds
The song of the birds, out of sight
Just beyond, farther in, farther in
You walk, curious, intrigued
Until you come to a clearing
In the distance you see a figure roaming around the clearing
It seems to be a boy or a young man, it is hard to tell which
Perhaps a boy exploring on a summer's day in the days before
    he becomes a man
You know this boy, you recognize the curiosity on his face
You can remember yourself in the space between boy and man
Wandering and wondering and dreaming and thinking long
    thoughts
The boy sits down to take a rest
You approach and sit across from him, he smiles welcoming
    you
His face holds the innocence of childhood and longing for an
    adventurous life
He lays back on the ground searching the sky
You lay next to him searching the sky
He tells you what he longs for, his dreams, his hopes and
    desires
What he hopes will happen in his life
Take the time now just to listen, listen to his vision
(3 minutes)

And with a deep sigh, the boy finishes
He sits up and you sit up across from him
You look into each other's eyes, deeply, deeply
A boy's will is the wind's will and the thoughts of youth are
    long, long thoughts
This boy's deep, long thoughts, hopes, dreams, values are
    yours
Your deep, long thoughts, hopes, dreams and values,
You remember these dreams of your youth
And standing, you say goodbye using only your eyes
And you find yourself in the woods, walking back from the
    clearing,
Walking back on the path,
Back to where you began
But now, remember the hopes and dreams of your youth
You gradually come back to the present,
And gradually, as you return you stretch
And stretching, open your eyes,
Finding yourself here in the room
Pick up your favorite pen
In your notebook or journal write down the hopes, and
    dreams you rediscovered.

Challenge Three: A Boy's Will

1. What wild memories lie deep within you about yourself
    as a boy or as a young man? Was there some experience
    (riding a bike down a steep hill, diving into a pool or
    pond, skateboarding) that you found exhilarating and
    you did it over and over? Did you ever feel like you were
    flying or escaping the earth?
2. Record these times in your journal and reflect on each of
    them. How did it feel? Did you get a 'rush?'
3. How did these experiences connect to your spirituality?

4. Make an abstract drawing or write a poem portraying the feeling.

Challenge Four: Dreaming and Connecting with Earth

In your youth you might have been told to stop your dreaming and come down to earth. Our practical parents, who had yet to become grandparents, might have enjoined us to view the world from a more earthly and reality based point of view. Now, as an Elder you are free to fuse the practical insights of your work and family-building life and go back and resuscitate those dreams and fulfill them in the new reality of life as a Vibrant Emeritus. List below a dream you had in your youth with the steps you might use to achieve it.

A Dream You Had:

Steps You Might Take to Achieve this Dream:

1.

2.

3.

4.

5.

6.

7.

A Poem to Contemplate

Birches
By Robert Frost

When I see birches bend to left and right
Across the lines of straighter darker trees,
I like to think some boy's been swinging them.
But swinging doesn't bend them down to stay
As ice-storms do. Often you must have seen them
Loaded with ice a sunny winter morning
After a rain. They click upon themselves
As the breeze rises, and turn many-colored
As the stir cracks and crazes their enamel.
Soon the sun's warmth makes them shed crystal shells
Shattering and avalanching on the snow-crust –
Such heaps of broken glass to sweep away
You'd think the inner dome of heaven had fallen.
They are dragged to the withered bracken by the load,
And they seem not to break; though once they are bowed
So low for long, they never right themselves:
You may see their trunks arching in the woods
Years afterwards, trailing their leaves on the ground
Like girls on hands and knees that throw their hair
Before them over their heads to dry in the sun.
But I was going to say when Truth broke in
With all her matter-of-fact about the ice-storm
I should prefer to have some boy bend them
As he went out and in to fetch the cows –
Some boy too far from town to learn baseball,
Whose only play was what he found himself,
Summer or winter, and could play alone.
One by one he subdued his father's trees
By riding them down over and over again

Until he took the stiffness out of them,
And not one but hung limp, not one was left
For him to conquer. He learned all there was
To learn about not launching out too soon
And so not carrying the tree away
Clear to the ground. He always kept his poise
To the top branches, climbing carefully
With the same pains you use to fill a cup
Up to the brim, and even above the brim.
Then he flung outward, feet first, with a swish,
Kicking his way down through the air to the ground.
So was I once myself a swinger of birches.
And so I dream of going back to be.
It's when I'm weary of considerations,
And life is too much like a pathless wood
Where your face burns and tickles with the cobwebs
Broken across it, and one eye is weeping
From a twig's having lashed across it open.
I'd like to get away from earth awhile
And then come back to it and begin over.
May no fate willfully misunderstand me
And half grant what I wish and snatch me away
Not to return. Earth's the right place for love:
I don't know where it's likely to go better.
I'd like to go by climbing a birch tree,
And climb black branches up a snow-white trunk
Toward heaven, till the tree could bear no more,
But dipped its top and set me down again.
That would be good both going and coming back.
One could do worse than be a swinger of birches.

Some Questions to Reflect Upon:

In the mundane world, the birches in the poem were likely to have been bent by a snowstorm. The poet prefers to believe that they were bent down a boy. The boy has no bounds and bends down all the available trees. What deep down desire might you have if you imagined yourself as a boundless boy?

The poet longs to return to the days when he was a "swinger of birches," unencumbered by the cares and concerns of his life. Where might you find your boundless boy? What time in your life might you want to relive?

While the poet imagines that he would like to launch himself from the Earth, he remembers that Earth is the right place for love. The poet, remembering this, asks to both expand his boundaries heavenward but then be brought back down to Earth. Where is the balance between the Vibrant Emeritus' desire to dream as he did as a boy and come back to earth to make love the center of his world?

Practices

1. Take some time for daydreaming and make it a regular part of your spiritual practice. Keep notes of the visions you have for yourself as an Elder, for those you love and those you mentor.
2. Review your notes and see how in reality you might promote those visions in your life and in the lives of others.

Growth Questions

Like innocent youth, the Elder years are a time to both dream freely and actualize without being bound by the conventions of the middle years. What dreams will I actualize?

Many men began in their Elder years to not only imagine but to fulfill their dreams by letting go of constraints and taking on new challenges that new freedom allows us to achieve. Robert Penn Warren, who as a young man won a Pulitzer Prize for his fiction, had a great burst of creativity in his seventies, winning another Pulitzer Prize for poetry. What burst of creativity and making might I have within me?

The Vibrant Emeritus has the opportunity to give back in his later years. What might I have to give?

Wisdom might be at the confluence of youthful dreams and noble vision and the practicality, skills and insight from living a lifetime. What is my wisdom?

Chapter 6

Deepening Spirituality

*I come to a turn in the road. I look around me. The world is splendid!
The world is animated with color and vibrant life! My spirit flies!
This is the fifth task.*

All this can feel like the wonder of aging rather than a scary sense of loss if we see it all as a cumulative new beginning, a rebirth. In that vein, we can ask, "Have I fulfilled my purpose? If not, what now? If so, will I have a new purpose? Even the debilitation of our bodies, inevitably a companion of aging, can feel liberating if we spend time (even a few years) digging deep into the self in order to decide what our second chances need to be. These second chances can happen in the relationships we are in or in our awakening to new passions and a new sense of adventure. They can happen as we enjoy our rites of passage into new stages of life and focus on becoming spiritually whole.

– Michael Gurian, *The Wonder of Aging*

The Task: Deepening Spirituality

The second half of our lives allows us to readjust our consciousness and focus on the way to wholeness we elect to follow. Author Drew Leder, writing about the awakening of the Buddha in his book *Spiritual Passages*, suggests:

In your own youth, someone may have tried to steer you down a certain path. Perhaps your parents wanted you to be a doctor, a lawyer, or an accountant, or to marry someone well-to-do. Or maybe the pressure came not so much from your parents as from the world at large. After all, everyone seems to value material success. The message screams at us from TV, magazines, advertising: "Have stuff, lots of stuff and you'll be happy. Pleasure, power, profit, prestige – that's the ticket!" We suck this message like baby food from the culture's breast. Sometimes it seems like we're force-fed it whether we're hungry or not.

Amidst all this pressure, maybe there were dreams we set aside. Siddhartha almost lost sight of his true calling. Maybe, to some degree, we have as well. Are there parts of the self that we left undeveloped? In our youth, did we feel drawn to something – the arts, nature, travel, spirituality – that we lost sight of along the way? Were there any life or career dreams that we abandoned? The great psychologist, Carl Jung, suggests that restrictive choices are inevitable in the first half of life as we build up the ego-self. We are seeking to define ourselves and succeed as individuals. But life's second half, he suggests, has a different purpose; we reach for psychospiritual wholeness. To do so, we need to develop the parts of ourselves that have been repressed or neglected. We need to honor what lies hidden within our souls.

When Wordsworth and Coleridge were investigating their response to the arrival of the Industrial Age and to the migration from village and farm to city, the horrible living conditions the men and women found there, the detachment humans suffered from the natural connection to the earth and spirit, each decided to take a different tact. Wordsworth decided to find spirituality from the mundane and make it seem fantastical. Coleridge went in the opposite direction, making the fantastic to appear available to all of us. Perhaps it is at the intersection of these two roads that spiritual oneness occurs.

Twice Parsifal is offered the opportunity to accept his deep masculine spirituality. The Legend of Parsifal is a Christian tale, a Grail Legend. The legend developed over many years. Over time the Grail became the chalice or wide plate transformed into the cup from the Last Supper and the cup used by Joseph of Arimathea to collect Christ's blood when he took him down from the cross and buried him after the crucifixion. In the Parsifal legend, as a young knight and later when he has finished his Warrior adventures, he is presented with the symbols of the Christian faith: the bloody lance that pierced Christ's chest, a golden paten used at communion, a candelabra, and the Grail itself. The grail has the power to transform.

As a youth, Parsifal is not ready to accept these symbols and embrace his full male spirituality. He is fairly feckless on his first visit, unaware of the significance of the opportunity. Having fully lived his adventurous life as a knight, he fully accepts these symbols, asks the crucial question "Whom does the Grail serve," and is crowned as the Grail King who is fully ready to use the grail as he heals the Fisher King, restores the wasteland to bounty, and rules the kingdom in righteousness. The Vibrant Emeritus, presented with this opportunity as one has aged to a time where one now understands the work of healing, of blessing and of giving, deepens one's spirituality to rule his realm with justice, fairness and abundance. This acceptance includes developing a deep spiritual practice and integrating one's life into this new stage of life.

A Classic Tale

Lines Composed a Few Miles above Tintern Abbey, On Revisiting the Banks of the Wye during a Tour. July 13, 1798
(By William Wordsworth)

Five years have past; five summers, with the length
Of five long winters! And again I hear
These waters, rolling from their mountain-springs
With a soft inland murmur. – Once again

Do I behold these steep and lofty cliffs,
That on a wild secluded scene impress
Thoughts of more deep seclusion; and connect
The landscape with the quiet of the sky.
The day is come when I again repose
Here, under this dark sycamore, and view
These plots of cottage-ground, these orchard-tufts,
Which at this season, with their unripe fruits,
Are clad in one green hue, and lose themselves
'Mid groves and copses. Once again I see
These hedge-rows, hardly hedge-rows, little lines
Of sportive wood run wild: these pastoral farms,
Green to the very door; and wreaths of smoke
Sent up, in silence, from among the trees!
With some uncertain notice, as might seem
Of vagrant dwellers in the houseless woods,
Or of some Hermit's cave, where by his fire
The Hermit sits alone.
These beauteous forms,
Through a long absence, have not been to me
As is a landscape to a blind man's eye:
But oft, in lonely rooms, and 'mid the din
Of towns and cities, I have owed to them,
In hours of weariness, sensations sweet,
Felt in the blood, and felt along the heart;
And passing even into my purer mind
With tranquil restoration: – feelings too
Of unremembered pleasure: such, perhaps,
As have no slight or trivial influence
On that best portion of a good man's life,
His little, nameless, unremembered acts
Of kindness and of love. Nor less, I trust,
To them I may have owed another gift,
Of aspect more sublime; that blessed mood,

In which the burthen of the mystery,
In which the heavy and the weary weight
Of all this unintelligible world,
Is lightened: – that serene and blessed mood,
In which the affections gently lead us on, –
Until, the breath of this corporeal frame
And even the motion of our human blood
Almost suspended, we are laid asleep
In body, and become a living soul:
While with an eye made quiet by the power
Of harmony, and the deep power of joy,
We see into the life of things.
If this
Be but a vain belief, yet, oh! How oft –
In darkness and amid the many shapes
Of joyless daylight; when the fretful stir
Unprofitable, and the fever of the world,
Have hung upon the beatings of my heart –
How oft, in spirit, have I turned to thee,
O sylvan Wye! Thou wanderer thro' the woods,
How often has my spirit turned to thee!

And now, with gleams of half-extinguished thought,
With many recognitions dim and faint,
And somewhat of a sad perplexity,
The picture of the mind revives again:
While here I stand, not only with the sense
Of present pleasure, but with pleasing thoughts
That in this moment there is life and food
For future years. And so I dare to hope,
Though changed, no doubt, from what I was when first
I came among these hills; when like a roe
I bounded o'er the mountains, by the sides
Of the deep rivers, and the lonely streams,

Wherever nature led: more like a man
Flying from something that he dreads, than one
Who sought the thing he loved. For nature then
(The coarser pleasures of my boyish days
And their glad animal movements all gone by)
To me was all in all. – I cannot paint
What then I was. The sounding cataract
Haunted me like a passion: the tall rock,
The mountain, and the deep and gloomy wood,
Their colours and their forms, were then to me
An appetite; a feeling and a love,
That had no need of a remoter charm,
By thought supplied, not any interest
Unborrowed from the eye. – That time is past,
And all its aching joys are now no more,
And all its dizzy raptures. Not for this
Faint I, nor mourn nor murmur; other gifts
Have followed; for such loss, I would believe,
Abundant recompense. For I have learned
To look on nature, not as in the hour
Of thoughtless youth; but hearing oftentimes
The still sad music of humanity,
Nor harsh nor grating, though of ample power
To chasten and subdue. – And I have felt
A presence that disturbs me with the joy
Of elevated thoughts; a sense sublime
Of something far more deeply interfused,
Whose dwelling is the light of setting suns,
And the round ocean and the living air,
And the blue sky, and in the mind of man:
A motion and a spirit, that impels
All thinking things, all objects of all thought,
And rolls through all things. Therefore am I still
A Lover of the meadows and the woods

And mountains; and of all that we behold
From this green earth; of all the mighty world
Of eye, and ear, – both what they half create,
And what perceive; well pleased to recognise
In nature and the language of the sense
The anchor of my purest thoughts, the nurse,
The guide, the guardian of my heart, and soul
Of all my moral being.
Nor perchance,
If I were not thus taught, should I the more
Suffer my genial spirits to decay:
For thou art with me here upon the banks
Of this fair river; thou my dearest Friend,
My dear, dear Friend; and in thy voice I catch
The language of my former heart, and read
My former pleasures in the shooting lights
Of thy wild eyes. Oh! Yet a little while
May I behold in thee what I was once,
My dear, dear Sister! And this prayer I make,
Knowing that Nature never did betray
The heart that loved her; 'tis her privilege,
Through all the years of this our life, to lead
From joy to joy: for she can so inform
The mind that is within us, so impress
With quietness and beauty, and so feed
With lofty thoughts, that neither evil tongues,
Rash judgments, nor the sneers of selfish men,
Nor greetings where no kindness is, nor all
The dreary intercourse of daily life,
Shall e'er prevail against us, or disturb
Our cheerful faith, that all which we behold
Is full of blessings. Therefore let the moon
Shine on thee in thy solitary walk;
And let the misty mountain-winds be free

To blow against thee: and, in after years,
When these wild ecstasies shall be matured
Into a sober pleasure; when thy mind
Shall be a mansion for all lovely forms,
Thy memory be as a dwelling-place
For all sweet sounds and harmonies; oh! Then,
If solitude, or fear, or pain, or grief,
Should be thy portion, with what healing thoughts
Of tender joy wilt thou remember me,
And these my exhortations! Nor, perchance –
If I should be where I no more can hear
Thy voice, nor catch from thy wild eyes these gleams
Of past existence – wilt thou then forget
That on the banks of this delightful stream
We stood together; and that I, so long
A worshipper of Nature, hither came
Unwearied in that service: rather say
With warmer love – oh! With far deeper zeal
Of holier love. Nor wilt thou then forget,
That after many wanderings, many years
Of absence, these steep woods and lofty cliffs,
And this green pastoral landscape, were to me
More dear, both for themselves and for thy sake!

Some Questions to Reflect Upon:

How do I master that which prevents me from going to my deep inner self?

Entering the deep soul of my nature, who am I?

How do I deepen and develop character?

In what ways do I bring true spirit, character, heart and authenticity?

Am I stuck in the past or racing to the future?

What is my next spiritual step?

A Contemporary Story: My Spirit Flies

I graduated from college in 1970. It had been a grueling four years of total unrest. Because I was a legacy, there was always for me the suspicion that I was not smart enough really to have attended such a high-grade university as Duke. I managed but graduated far down at the bottom of my class. I had been involved in all the exciting and adventurous elements that marked the Sixties. I had raged against the system and the insanity of the Vietnam War. I eschewed liquor but embraced whatever chemicals were available, and whatever effects they had on the consciousness, gladly. In order to graduate, I had to earn the highest grades of the four years, and I did. By spring I was exhausted, depleted and scared of leaving school forever (or what seemed forever).

There was a call to march again on Washington, and the university allowed students to take the grades they had achieved so far in their classes and go again to march. I took this opportunity but I did not march as I had three times before. My roommate and I rented a tent and drove to the Outer Banks. The further away we drove from Durham, the deeper we breathed, the more the Outer Banks seemed an exotic destination. Driving off the ferry, we entered an enchantment that lasted as long as we stayed. We had a supply of LSD under the impression that dropping acid would enhance greatly our experiences on the wild and windy sand dunes. We never used it. We camped at a primitive campsite provided by the National Seashore.

The first afternoon we pitched the tent, took hikes and slept under the burning sun. Evening came and, as night fell, other campers carried tables down to the shoreline and lighted hurricane lamps. I remembered the words of my favorite poet,

Wallace Stevens, who wrote them at another beach further south:

Oh! Blessed rage for order, pale Ramon,
The maker's rage to order words of the sea,
Words of the fragrant portals, dimly-starred,
And of ourselves and of our origins,
In ghostlier demarcations, keener sounds.

The night sky was as deep and illuminated with an ocean of stars as I have ever experienced. There came upon us a kind of enchantment as we danced in the waves, and naked, dove into the ocean. We were exhilarated, as the moon rose giving the beach a soft sheen until it faded and the hurricane lamps marked out the darkness.

We slept as the moon rose and we rose as the sun crept over the sea. One morning, my roomie and I just started walking along the beach toward the sunrise. At first the sky was Homer's rosy tipped sky and then the sun, brilliant and big, arose over the water, and we walked and walked silent until it rose fully. That time is anchored in my memory as deeply spiritual and deeply connected to myself, to my friend, to the ocean, to the universe, to spirit.

Carrying that memory I have had a series of similar times of spiritual connection in nature – on Prince Edward Island, on the Pacific at Monterey, Whiskey Beach, at Big Sur, in Eureka, at Yellowstone, at Yosemite, and on Cape Cod, each of them linked, woven into a fabric of ecstatic moments, one building on the other.

Two summers ago, I spent a day at Scituate Harbor, Massachusetts. Scituate is especially meaningful to me because my ancestors, the Stetsons, built their first homes there. On this day I went out on some boulders beyond the lighthouse and meditated for four to five hours under the fat sun. The same sun that warms the Outer Banks, Prince Edward Island, Yellowstone,

Yosemite, Big Sur, Whiskey Beach, and Monterey. It was here on the rocks under the sun, out on the thrust into the sea, I accepted the challenges of becoming a Vibrant Emeritus, of exploring what that would mean, and putting together trainings, training materials and a book describing this phase of life as a crucial part of life not only for one's self, but for one's family, and one's community.

I often meditate and sometimes I return to the breath of wind passing over my body, the full rays of the sun burning my skin, the feel of sand or rock under my back, the endless sound of waves; and when I do, I feel that old connection that connects me to all that was, is or will be. When I write these words, it sometimes feels as though I am downloading or taking dictation from a higher source from deep within my consciousness. I am writing from a deep spiritual place.

Discussion

Many men and women find spiritual connection within their religious faith. I can remember several times when I was deeply moved by attending Roman Catholic Mass, especially when I attended an African-American Catholic church. The combination of drumming and singing spirituals and the emotion of the congregation deeply touched my heart, and connected my soul with God. I have also had deep experiences during the Easter Mass at Midnight at the Benedictine monastery of Saint Meinrad in Indiana.

I have talked with musicians who describe a similar connection when playing their chosen musical instrument. They speak of entering into the music and being carried away to a deeply spiritual place. Very few persons do not feel the grandeur of a greater power in nature, by an ocean or waterfall, deep in the woods, walking among the redwoods, at sunrise and sunset.

Could we endure overwhelming experiences daily? Or, does the view dull. I often wonder if people who live overlooking seascapes and mountaintops still find the ecstasies the pilgrim enjoys. Between these experiences lies practice.

Challenges

Challenge One: Writing Your Story

1. Reflect on the classic tale of *Tintern Abbey* and think about its themes, its use of archetypes, and its perspectives on growth, change, and healing.
2. Reflect on the contemporary story and how it connects with the classic tale.
3. Reflect on when your spirit flies. Write your own contemporary story.

Challenge Two: My Spirit Flies Visualization

1. Either read the following visualization into a recorder so that you can play it to yourself or ask a person you trust to read it to you. Make sure to pause for ten seconds between each line.
2. Place a favorite pen and notebook or journal near to the place where you are visualizing.
3. Playing soft, meditative music can enhance the experience.
4. Follow the direction of the visualization narrative:

I invite you to lie on the floor on your back and get comfortable. Find a place where you feel alone.

When you are ready, I invite you to close your eyes.

Take a deep cleansing breath, that is, breathe in through your nose, hold the breath and then slowly release the breath through your mouth. Let's do this together,

Take a deep breath filling your lungs for a count of 10, hold your breath for a count of 10, then release slowly for a count of 10.

Now I invite you to breathe normally, deeply, slowly, and concentrate on the breath coming in and flowing out.

As you slowly breathe in, imagine that you are allowing a deep white light to enter your head. It is beautiful, healing and relaxing light.

The light fills your body and flows into your head and out through your toes.

As you will with light, your body relaxes. You continue to breathe very deeply.

You feel your body sink into the floor.

Any tension you might hold flow out.

The healing and relaxing light flows through you through your deep breathing.

Notice where you might hold any tension and let it go.

In your neck, in your shoulders.

Let it go.

In your arms and hands.

Let it go

In your chest and stomach

Let it go

In your hips and thighs

Let it go

In your calves, ankles or feet

Any tension,

Let it go

Breathe deeply and let it go

Let it go until you feel like you are floating,

You might feel like you are floating on a comfortable raft

It feels so nice, the gentle rocking of the raft as it floats gently on the water.

The day is bright, the sun feels warm on your body, a perfect day, floating

Gentle breezes touch your skin, your face

Floating on the water, a gentle back and forth of the gentle
waves

Floating, you and the raft are one, your body so comfortable,
the gentle rock

Of the water, back and forth gently,

You feel yourself floating and gently moving on the water

Back and forth; back and forth; back and forth

Only the sound of the water and gentle breeze

Back and forth; back and forth; back and forth;

Gently floating, moving in the easy current

Toward a place you've been to sometime before

A welcoming place; a place somewhere in time

Somewhere in memory; your memory; deeply remembered;

And easily you come to rest in this place

Under the welcoming sun; still the welcoming breezes

You find yourself in this safe place somewhere deep in
memory

And you stand easily and look around

The colors you see are amazing

As though they were animated and vibrating

Brilliant, amazing; welcoming

Look around you until you see a path,

The path is intriguing and you want to follow

a path leading into the vibrant landscape

Away from the water and the shore and the sun

Deeper in;

deeper in;

deeper in

you walk deeper in

Into the vibrancy of all around you

It is a journey you want to take

A place you want to go and go to with ever-increasing joy

It feels amazingly safe and amazingly dangerous and you

want to go further
And with each step deeper into the vibrancy
You feel a presence at first, a breath's whisper
The gentle breathing of someone you know quite well
Who has been there always just beyond what you see and
hear and feel
But present and safe and comforting and adventurous
Ready
To protect
Ready to explore
Ready to risk
The newness you are walking toward
You will know the place,
The presence beside you walking
In sync with you takes the form of light
Of a personage you are quite familiar with because
It is a presence always present,
Perhaps a guide
Perhaps a master,
Perhaps the higher you;
Perhaps your soul
Walking with this presence you feel at one, together,
Walking together until you come to the place you have been
yearning for
That you have always known and know now for the first time
And knowing it now you and the presence sit together by a
still lake
The sun on the water causing a kind of path of light across the
water
That comes from the light that flows from deep within you
And from above and towards forever
And here in this place of solitude and connection
Connection to the vibrancy that abounds all around you
And the stillness of the water and the path

Connected to this other and connected to your self
You sit in silence and wait
Wait until what was; what is; what is to be
Settles in the stillness and the silence
(2 minutes of silence)

Here you know who you are and why you are
And the other presence who is your presence
Whispers softly in your ear
(2 minutes of silence)

These words are words you will remember
Words of guidance, truth and direction
Listen again
(2 minutes of silence)

Find a place on your body to anchor these words
This revelation
(1 minute)

Standing you face this well-known, now remembered self
You embrace, breathing into you this presence
Who has been, is and always will be with you
Who you can be with whenever you sit in silence
And anchor to this place
This place of the deeply masculine
This place of the Spirit; the deeply masculine spirit
That lives always with you and who comes to you
When you come to this place
Just as you lay down for sleep;
Just as you awaken;
When you sit still and listen
When in the silence you listen again to this deep, spiritual,
    masculine voice

That awaits under the chatter of the day to day
At this vibrant place that now you know the way to
Standing to face this person and look deeply into his loving
 eyes
Embrace and feel the strength of his body against yours
And gradually take in one another into your skin
And feel the love and the joy of this fusion
The strength, the protection, the fear and the risk
The vibrancy, and breathe into you the vibrancy
Of the wild and precious life all around you and within you
And know this place
It is the place where you come to be grounded
It is the still point in the dance
Where the end is the beginning and the beginning the end
And at this still point the fulcrum of your life
You find yourself floating again on the gentle waters
The waters of life that brought you here
And again you feel the gentle forth and back and forth and
 back
Of the raft on the water your body one with the raft
Under the fat sun and gentle breeze
The sun feels so good on your body and face
The breeze feels so good on your body and face
As you drift forth and back on the water; on the raft
And over the next few moments you drift
Until the raft slows and stops
And the movement of the water ends
And gradually the raft becomes the floor
And gradually you come back to the room
Very gradually and in your own time
Remembering all you experienced
Remembering the presence of the presence within you
And knowing that today
The rest of the day you will be serene

And happy and connected to yourself
And to the others you meet and see
For you know that we are all one
And all is one
Drifting back into the room
Until you are fully back and you know
It is time to breathe deeply and open your eyes gradually
And feel the solidity of the floor beneath you
And taking a long and easy stretch you
Move into a sitting position
And stretching again look around you
Pick up your favorite pen
In your notebook or journal make notes of your experience.

Challenge Three: When Does My Spirit Fly?

1. Select a large sheet of drawing paper and gather crayons, markers or watercolors.
2. Select some soft music to play in the background.
3. Breathe deep and think about a time or place where your spirit flies.
4. Gradually draw either realistically or abstractly the place/time where your spirit flies.
5. With a trusted friend or partner, describe to each other where you feel deeply connected to spirit.

Challenge Four: How do I Express My Spirituality?

1. There are many ways to enhance our souls and express to ourselves and others our spiritual foundation.
2. Consider a way to express yourself in making art, writing, journaling, singing, listening to music or some other expression.
3. After a session where you meditate, contemplate or use

some other spiritual approach, use a method of expression to express your spirituality. Some people find that doing the art or expression can become the spiritual practice.

A Poem to Contemplate

God's Grandeur
By Gerard Manley Hopkins

The world is charged with the grandeur of God.
It will flame out, like shining from shook foil;
It gathers to a greatness, like the ooze of oil
Crushed. Why do men then now not reck his rod?
Generations have trod, have trod, have trod;
And all is seared with trade; bleared, smeared with toil;
And wears man's smudge and shares man's smell: the soil
Is bare now, nor can foot feel, being shod.

And for all this, nature is never spent;
There lives the dearest freshness deep down things;
And though the last lights off the black West went
Oh, morning, at the brown brink eastward, springs –
Because the Holy Ghost over the bent
World broods with warm breast and with ah! Bright wings.

Some Questions to Reflect Upon:

What 'charges' your world?

How do you imagine your 'Higher Power?'

What is your connection with Nature?

How do you refresh your world?

Practices

1. There are many ways up the spiritual mountain. Find the one that most appeals to you, your lifestyle, and appears to work for you. This can be a formal practice or one of your own devising.
2. Some form of daily meditation might be very useful to you.
3. Many people find a spiritual director useful, someone who asks the right questions to influence your spiritual growth.
4. Taking spiritual vacations to an ashram, monastery or retreat center can help one spiritually refocus.

Growth Questions

When or where do I feel most spiritually connected with myself and with what I consider my higher power?

How might I develop a consistent practice of meditation and prayer?

What deepens me spiritually?

How might I measure if I am growing spiritually?

How does my spirituality connect with all the other tasks of the Vibrant Emeritus?

Chapter 7

Mentoring the Next Generation

I come to place in the road where I feel within myself a noble challenge.
I ask myself: What will I give? What will I create? Whom will I serve?
What is my legacy?
This is the sixth task.

That's why an Elder's heart leaps up when a younger person says, "Please take me on as your student or apprentice. There's so much I want to learn from you."
– Zalman Schachter-Shalomi

The Task: Mentoring the Next Generation

The sixth task is the ongoing task of mentoring the next generation. The task is marked by listening, encouraging, suggesting, relating, challenging, role-modeling, and inspiring. When a younger man asks an Elder to teach him something, to just hang together and talk, to share a common interest, to be a sounding board, or for a blessing, it is the honor for the Elder to be asked to become a mentor. It is not the younger person's honor to have the Elder as a mentor, even though the mentee usually respects, and perhaps loves, the mentor. The best mentoring is ego-free, selfless, and focused on the requests of the mentee. The greatest mentors are humble and not attached to the choices or learning of the mentee. That is, the mentee takes from the relationship that which he feels he needs. While the mentor hopes for the success of the mentee and his decisions, he allows the mentee to fail, but does not gloat if what the mentor suggested might be a better choice. It is the mentee's job to discover from experience, reflection and discussion with the mentor. Great mentors use the Socratic questioning method by listening rather than telling, suggesting rather than demanding, and honoring and blessing the younger man.

In the Legend of Parsifal, the mentor presented is Gournamond. In his book *Quest for the Grail*, Richard Rohr explains the role of the mentor as embodied in Gournamond this way:

> On his way [Parsifal] finds this castle.
>
> In the castle, he meets the one we would call his godfather. Gournamond is the name given him in some versions of the legend. We get the impression Parsifal lives with him for some time. This is the castle of masculinity, the castle where the godfather, the goodfather, teaches the boy. It is a symbol of initiation. Very often, especially if the son had an abusive father who either physically or verbally abused him or emotionally demeaned him in any way, there is a desperate need in the boy for a godfather.
>
> The godfather tradition did not develop by accident but because it was needed...
>
> Parsifal comes to the castle of the good father, the one who is going to take care of him, the 'male mother,' so to speak. Normally, as a man grows up, there is a bonding with the mother, then the break with the mother. He breaks with the father, when he discovers another male father, a coach, a hero, a mentor.
>
> Finally, after Parsifal has worked at the castle and been trained there by Gournamond, he takes off his mother's homespun clothes. Finally he has an authentic male relationship and his own male identity! Gournamond teaches him how to wear the armor and ride the horse and especially how to stop it. Heretofore, he did not know how to stop the horse, how to set limits to his own phallic drives. Most important, Gournamond teaches him the crucial question to be asked at the appropriate time: "One day you are going to come upon a great castle, bigger than my castle. It will be the

Grail castle, and when you get there, remember only to ask one question."

Elders pass on the wisdom, knowledge, specialized skills, traditions, folklore, arts and crafts, stories and legends, and spiritual experience of the community. It is a relationship of renewal for the culture. Together with the mentee, that lore, knowledge and skill is often refined, transmuted and adapted in ways that make sense and enrich the developing new insights and beliefs that the younger generation are making. It is a relationship where the Elders' generativity refreshes, renews and replenishes the culture of the community.

Traditionally, it was the Elders who initiated youth into men, men into Warriors, and Warriors into Elders. The Elders bestowed the markings, the wounds, and the emblem of the new status to the initiated. Because the survival of the commonly held culture was in the hands of the Elders, Elders were generally sought after for counsel of individuals, and when communities made decisions.

Since the Industrial Revolution that turned thousands of years of human history topsy-turvy and destroyed the wisdom, culture, governance, rites and rituals of the communities that had been the domestic way of life since the Agrarian Revolution, the Elder has lost his honored and trusted position. In fact, the Elder is seen as the living image of the dissipating, aging, disempowered and dying figure many men and women contemplate becoming in the last half of life. It is an image that frightens and chills the souls of men as they begin to age and consider what the meaning and purpose of the last half of life means for them.

Mentoring (as well as the Elder Work of the other seven tasks of the Elder) when well-done can reincarnate the relationship of the Elder to his people, between younger and older, as a time of life that naturally ought to be revered, honored, respected and looked forward to among younger men as they age. The Vibrant Emeritus is the embodiment of such an Elder who enriches, blesses, and gives from the lifetime abundance one has brought about to his community. In this communal space the Elder is not shunned or left in isolation but becomes the center of the community life.

A Classic Tale

An Old Man's Wisdom
(An Indian Folktale)

In a country far away there was a farmer who had tilled the soil for many years cultivating rice. He was the oldest man in the village; he lived quietly with his grandson at the edge of the village close to his rice fields. Occasionally, a younger man would approach him and ask him for his insights and opinions.

"Keep your fields clear of weeds and cultivate a good crop."

The younger men would shake their heads as they left, for their heads were filled with visions of the wild hunt, of the wild fruits of the wilderness, and of chasing down animals to their death. They heeded the call to adventure and they left their fields to the women to tend. But the work of the women could not make up for the work of the men and soon the fields were tangled with weeds, choking out the tender plants.

One day the old man's grandson said, "Grandfather, I long to follow the men into the forests to hunt and to fish with them."

"Do this, my grandson. Go to the river and take this coin to the fishermen working there. Bring back to me a small fish still alive."

The boy found a fishing net and did as Grandfather asked. When he returned, Grandfather said, "Now, boy, go to the pig pen and fetch me a trough used for feeding the pigs."

This the boy did and Grandfather filled the wooden trough with water, dropping the fish into the trough.

"Now bring me that fish and we will cook it for our supper."

The boy thought, "Why is Grandfather giving me such an easy task? This is dull and boring!"

But soon his fishing in the trough was not dull and boring but frustrating and fruitless. Try as he might, he could not grab the fish and bring it to his grandfather.

"My dear grandson, if you cannot fish successfully in this wooden trough, how do you expect to survive from fishing in the wild streams of the forest? Let us turn our attention to the rice in our fields. Let us do everything possible to insure a bumper crop. I understand that compared to the hunt and the chase and life in the forest this seems tiresome and frustrating, but I promise that the meats, fruits and riches of the earth will come to us."

"But how, Grandfather?"

"You will see in time."

Grandfather taught the knowledge regarding cultivating the fields he had gained over a lifetime of successful farming. And as they worked together, Grandfather answered all the questions the boy's highly curious mind could imagine. Grandfather loved the boy, was very patient, listened deeply, and calmly explained his insights, wonder, and understanding of life. The boy stayed intrigued all summer, and when harvest time came, Grandfather and the boy yielded a crop twice the size of their usual annual yield.

"You see, boy, we have far more than what you and I will need to survive this winter."

"But, Grandfather, you said we would have venison and boar, yams and wild berries, and a bounty of fish!"

"Be patient, it will come."

For the other villagers, the yield of their crops was poor. But the hunt was successful and they held great feasts celebrating their triumph. But as the days passed after the feasts, it became apparent that soon they would be out of rice, the staple of their lives. Soon, the villagers came to Grandfather, willing to trade the wild vegetables and fruits, the game and the fish in exchange for rice.

Now Grandfather and the boy could vary their diet as they had plenty throughout the long winter.

As they ate a small feast one night, Grandfather said to the boy, "Do you see, my grandson, the wisdom of our approach to life? Do you understand the magic we worked so we did not hunt nor fish but our larders are full of meat and game? Do you see that if we take care of the basics of life, all else falls into place?"

Over time, the villagers realized the wisdom of Grandfather. Soon, they too cultivated rice and tended to their fields. The years of famine ended. The earth bloomed. Abundance flowed.

A Contemporary Story

Mr. Miyagi

In the mid-1980s, I began helping schools and communities implement mentoring programs to foster positive youth development and a concept called "resiliency." The "resiliency researchers," such as Emmy Werner and Bonnie Benard and, later, the Search Institute found that children who had "protective factors" in their lives were more likely to survive and thrive after some sort of trauma in their lives (an alcoholic family, a parent with cancer, a family member with mental illness, poverty, a dangerous neighborhood) than children who, facing the same traumas, did not have similar factors in their lives. The key protective factor was having positive role model adults in their lives, usually adults from outside the nuclear family, quite often a teacher, counselor, coach, youth worker, extended family member, or other adult who acted as a mentor in the life of a child.

Mentors were not parent replacements, but men and women who would listen deeply, answer authentically, allow the young person to discover answers for himself or herself, honor and celebrate the young person's accomplishments, and when an appropriate time came, dissolve the relationship.

A number of schools asked me to help them create an effective program especially for children who might need extra support or who came from single parent homes. The schools invited men and women to become a part of a mentoring pool. Many of these adults had no children or had raised families or felt called to work with youth. I would offer these volunteers training in one-to-one communication skills, coaching skills and define the mentoring relationship. Then I would facilitate a day-long experience where the mentor/mentee relationship would begin to form.

At that time, the film *The Karate Kid* was very popular and I often used it as an example of excellent mentoring. It tells the story of a boy who moves to California from New Jersey. Daniel appears awkward and clueless and quickly becomes the target of bullies. The leading bully is the ex-boyfriend of a cheerleader who befriends Daniel. The local bullies are students at a dojo run by an ex-Special Forces Vietnam veteran, John Kreese. This shadowy sensei eschews the traditional values of mercy and restraint, promoting vicious attacks and bullying behavior in his young students.

One day, Daniel takes a beating from the bullies, witnessed by the apartment handyman where Daniel lives, Mr. Miyagi. Mr. Miyagi intervenes, single-handedly defeating the gang of bullies. At a meeting with Sensei Kreese, Mr. Miyagi agrees to have Daniel ready to fight at a karate tournament and gets the sensei to agree to call off the bullying while Daniel trains. Mr. Miyagi becomes Daniel's mentor in both karate and in life situations.

The mentor's methods confuse and frustrate Daniel. Instead of teaching him specific moves at first, he assigns him menial tasks such as waxing a car (the famous "wax on/wax off" scene). Finally Mr. Miyagi demonstrates how each of the tasks has trained Daniel's body to naturally use the essential movements it takes to develop the technical skills of the fighting moves. As training continues, the bonding between Daniel and his mentor deepens and Daniel learns about the personal life of Mr. Miyagi – including losing his wife and son at childbirth in an internment camp for Japanese-Americans and his winning the medal of honor for his courageous fighting in Europe during World War II.

Despite ruthless and illegal moves demanded by the Sensei Kreese disabling Daniel, he moves round after round until the title match. One boy disables his leg. Later his challenger illegally sweeps Daniel's injured leg. Using a move Daniel has secretly practiced after observing his mentor, the "Crane Movement," Daniel wins the championship at the last minute of the match.

I have had a number of mentors in my life who have inspired me and seen things in me I did not see in myself.

In college at Duke University two professors challenged me, widened my horizons and changed my life: a professor of Italian Renaissance history, Frederick Krantz, and American literature professor John Clum.

As a young teacher I was inspired by the Reverend Frank Cayce who was Headmaster of Saint Francis School in Goshen, Kentucky. Frank had never been a principal and was an Episcopal priest. He was unafraid of new ideas and experimenting with new educational concepts. The school he created believed in core concepts that all children could learn at the highest levels if approached individually with the right teaching techniques; that it was the teacher's job to build positive relationships with their students; and personal development was as important as academic development, and both could be achieved simultaneously. I learned from Frank to follow my own ideas and to dare to take on challenges even when I had no experience in that field. I became a master curriculum developer for adolescents.

Leon Hisle became president of Our Lady of Bellefonte Hospital in Russell, Kentucky. He invited me to become the Executive Director of the hospital's chemical dependency treatment center, a small hospital located on the Bellefonte campus, to manage the adult unit and build an adolescent treatment program – even though my only experience had been as a teacher. Through this experience I learned the ways of business, program management, and marketing.

Wayne Hunnicutt, president of National Training Associates, made a place for me on his staff of master trainers. Under his mentorship, I was able to rise to the top of the training profession, develop new techniques of facilitation and presentation, and become a professional author and program developer. Like Frank and Leon, he was a visionary leader who created new, positive and inspiring institutions and companies based on life-changing principles.

When I began to consciously focus on my own Vibrant Emeritus years, I began to connect with men who asked me to be their mentor. It was not my intent and, in fact, I had told the chairman of the mentoring program for the MKP of Kentucky that I would not entertain being a mentor. I used my recent kidney transplant as an excuse. Within a month, I was approached by a young man who asked if I would consider mentoring him. Several of the men I have had the honor to serve are in their late twenties to mid-thirties. I was also asked by an older man developing a career in facilitation and presentation skills as well as several men pursuing leadership skills.

Through my interactions with my mentees, I have been taught to be a skilled and sensitive mentor. Unlike Mr. Miyagi, I have had to learn these skills from my mentees: to listen carefully, to reflect honestly, to answer authentically, to suggest rather than tell, to read body language, and to be of service to them rather than myself.

Discussion

In traditional societies, as the classic tale from India infers, Elders as mentors were common, natural and expected. It is the grandfather not the father teaching his grandson how to survive and thrive. It is a story of attraction in that ultimately the villagers come to the grandfather and boy in order to receive the staff of life. Like Mr. Miyagi, the grandfather does not tell nor directly teach but through a sequence of seemingly counterintuitive exercises and experiences, the boy and Daniel learn. What is learned goes against the common wisdom. Others in the village went to fish and gather fruits – a more exciting way of gathering food. The other boys go to a glitzy dojo where the Sensei teaches them directly from a place of control. In fact, Kreese controls them like puppets, telling them what to do and instructing them to cheat and practice illegal moves.

The great mentor is gentle, allows the mentee to fail and learn from his failure, encourages, and makes the mundane magical. He asks the mentee to wait for the final outcome; and role models in his own life the core values, practices and values he wants to impart, and he models high ideals. The bond between mentor and mentee is not parental, but deeply respectful on both sides of the relationship.

Challenges

Challenge One: Writing Your Story

1. Reflect on the classic tale of *An Old Man's Wisdom* and think about its themes, its use of archetypes, and its perspectives on growth, change, and healing.
2. Reflect on the contemporary story, and how it connects with the classic tale.
3. Reflect on mentors in your life. Write your own contemporary story.

Challenge Two: Whom Do I Serve? How do I Serve Myself? How Do I Serve Others?

1. Use markers and a large piece of chart paper.
2. Divide the sheet of paper from top to bottom equally.
3. On the left side, identify individuals or organizations you might serve in a mentoring capacity.
4. How will you serve yourself physically? Emotionally? Spiritually?
5. List specific ways how you might use your mentoring skills.

Challenge Three: What do I Bring to the Picnic?

1. Work with a partner.
2. Take a dinner-sized paper plate and thin colored markers.
3. Brainstorm randomly skills, talents, experiences, practices and knowledge that might be useful to a younger person.
4. Write them as they occur to you.
5. In one color, circle all the skills you might pass on to a younger man or woman.
6. In another color, circle all the talents you might pass on to a younger man or woman.
7. In another color, circle all the practices you have found useful in your life.
8. In another color, circle any special categories of knowledge you possess.
9. Using the paper plate, discuss with your partner what you bring to the picnic as a mentor for the next generation.

Challenge Four: A Letter to Your Mentor

1. Many successful people have had at many times of their lives teachers, coaches, older friends and mentors who

supported them. Brainstorm and make a list of any person from the time you were a boy who influenced you, provided you with insights, trained you in a skill, coached you, or supported you in some positive way.

2. Use your own stationery or design stationery that represents you as a man.

3. Write a letter to each of your mentors in which you thank them for their influence in your life. Describe to them how they influenced you and how you are still influenced by them in your life.

4. If they are alive, send the letter to them.

5. If they are deceased, send the letter to one of their relatives who might appreciate hearing how their relative influenced your life.

A Poem to Contemplate

Wisdom
By Sara Teasdale

When I have ceased to break my wings
Against the faultiness of things,
And learned that compromises wait
Behind each hardly opened gate,
When I have looked Life in the eyes,
Grown calm and very coldly wise,
Life will have given me the Truth,
And taken in exchange – my youth.

Some Questions to Reflect Upon:

What wisdom have you learned from life to pass on?

Is your wisdom positive, negative, jaded, optimistic, or inspiring?

Is wisdom a fair exchange for youth?

What compromises, if any, would you recommend to the young?

Is wisdom drawn from experience always cold?

Practices

1. In most communities there are opportunities to mentor youth. Big Brothers/Big Sisters offers an intense experience. Other community services often need responsible adults to help out including reading to children, aiding in schools, or serving the disabled. Check out the agency that fits you.
2. There are also adult possibilities in nursing homes, offering tax services, or providing mentoring in an area that you have expertise. Check these out to see if they fit.

Growth Questions

The change in consciousness from the Warrior life to the Elder life is a change from inward oriented, ego-driven pursuits, challenges, and achievements to letting go of ego and serving others. How might mentoring others help me change my conscious focus?

There is a danger in mentoring others in that one might continue the pursuit of ego-driven pursuits in the guise of helping and serving. Mentoring from this perspective is a type of manipulation. True service provides positive influence. The distinction can be discerned by asking oneself honestly and ruthlessly, "Who is this for?"

What are the most effective ways for communicating with my mentee? How often am I truly listening?

Am I listening and reflecting, and allowing my mentee to figure things out on his or her own?

Am I suggesting rather than telling my mentee what I think he or she ought to know?

What are the satisfactions and blessings I receive from a mentoring relationship?

Chapter 8

Dying Consciously

I come to a stopping place. The view ahead is dim. It is time to rest. I ask myself: Am I fulfilled? Can I let go? Will I find peace?
This is the final task.

Life is a quest whose last days can be lived in conflict and fear, even loneliness, for both the one dying and the family and culture around the one dying, or it can be a quest whose last days are lived in the purest love. It can be a few timeless moments of family history lived together, charged with energy, that help us all realize life's great plan: love. It can be a time of resolution when the one dying is allowed, through support and ease of his or her family and society, to see that what we give in our lifetimes has been substantial. This resolution can make our death very beautiful. In this beauty, we who will survive the dead are already grieving but the grief is beautiful, too, for it opens our souls like intense therapy, naturally accomplished.

– Michael Gurian, *The Wonder of Aging*

The Task

The Buddha gave up his corporeal manifestation, leaving his body and entering *parinirvana*. On the cross, Jesus commended his spirit unto his Father. Saint Francis embraced Sister Death. In each case the spiritual leader moved to a higher spiritual state consciously, achieving freedom, and initiating into a new consciousness. Mohammed chose union with God over this life when offered the choice.

The final task is the ultimate letting go of all things from this life. It can be a time to fully embrace who we are. Michael Gurian writes in *The Wonder of Aging*:

> Our dying and our death complete us; thus they are by nature
> a part of the completion spiritually we are developing (even if
> unconsciously) in our last decades of life, and then, in deep
> concentration, the final years or months of life. This
> completion involves our seeing the self as the sum of its parts
> – an accumulation of relationships, memories, and accom-
> plishments in our life – a 'sum' that still has its purpose:
> service to others. I believe we become most free in our dying
> and death when we remain in service to the world, to the very
> end. In this concentration and devotion, our personal feelings
> are ours, as sacred and private as we wish; and we do not
> either withhold them too much or show them so much that we
> manipulate and overwhelm others with our fears.

Rabbi Zalman Schachter-Shalomi recommends facing one's death
consciously and embracing its adventure:

> We will reap great rewards for this preparation, not only
> when pushing off from death's promontory, but throughout
> the remainder of our days. For by confronting death in life, we
> come out of hiding and open our hearts to the human
> community… At the same time, we put aside our proud but
> pathological sense of separateness and give up the deadening,
> habitual ways of living that the spiritual traditions call sleep.
> Interdependent with the greater web of life and brimming
> with sensory vitality, we will no longer postpone our
> engagement with life. By confronting death we finally will
> learn the art of living.

A Classic Tale

Godfather Death

(Grimm's Fairy Tales)

A poor man had twelve children and had to work day and night in order just to feed them. Thus when the thirteenth came into the world, not knowing what to do in his need, he ran out into the highway, intending to ask the first person whom he met to be the godfather.

The first person who came his way was our dear God, who already knew what was in his heart, and God said to him, "Poor man, I pity you. I will hold your child at his baptism, and care for him, and make him happy on earth." The man said, "Who are you?" – "I am God." – "Then I do not wish to have you for a godfather," said the man. "You give to the rich, and let the poor starve." Thus spoke the man, for he did not know how wisely God divides out wealth and poverty. Then he turned away from the Lord, and went on his way.

Then the devil came to him and said, "What are you looking for? If you will take me as your child's godfather, I will give him an abundance of gold and all the joys of the world as well." The man asked, "Who are you?" – "I am the devil." – "Then I do not wish to have you for a godfather," said the man. "You deceive mankind and lead them astray."

He went on his way, and then Death, on his withered legs, came walking toward him, and said, "Take me as your child's godfather." The man asked, "Who are you?" – "I am Death, who makes everyone equal." Then the man said, "You are the right one. You take away the rich as well as the poor, without distinction. You shall be my child's godfather. Death answered, "I will make your child rich and famous, for he who has me for a friend cannot fail." The man said, "Next Sunday is the baptism. Be there on time." Death appeared as he had promised, and served as godfather in an orderly manner.

After the boy came of age his godfather appeared to him one day and asked him to go with him. He took him out into the woods and showed him an herb that grew there, saying, "Now you shall receive your godfather's present. I will turn you into a famous physician. Whenever you are called to a sick person I will appear to you. If I stand at the sick person's head, you may say with confidence that you can make him well again; then give him some of this herb, and he will recover. But if I stand at the sick person's feet, he is mine, and you must say that he is beyond help, and that no physician in the world could save him. But beware of using this herb against my will, or something very bad will happen to you."

It was not long before the young man had become the most famous physician in the whole world. People said of him, "He only needs to look at the sick in order to immediately know their condition, whether they will regain their health, or are doomed to die." And people came to him from far and wide, taking him to their sick, and giving him so much money that he soon became a wealthy man.

Now it came to pass that the king became ill. The physician was summoned and was told to say if a recovery were possible. However, when he approached the bed, Death was standing at the sick man's feet, and so no herb on earth would be able to help him. "If I could only deceive death for once," thought the physician. "He will be angry, of course, but because I am his godson he will shut one eye. I will risk it."

He therefore took hold of the sick man and laid him the other way around, so that Death was now standing at his head. Then he gave the king some of the herb, and he recovered and became healthy again. However, Death came to the physician, made a dark and angry face, threatened him with his finger, and said, "You have betrayed me. I will overlook it this time because you are my godson, but if you dare to do it again, it will cost you your neck, for I will take you yourself away with me."

Soon afterward the king's daughter became seriously ill. She was his only child, and he cried day and night until his eyes were going blind. Then he proclaimed that whosoever rescued her from death should become her husband and inherit the crown. When the physician came to the sick girl's bed he saw Death at her feet. He should have remembered his godfather's warning, but he was so infatuated by the princess' great beauty and the prospect of becoming her husband that he threw all thought to the winds. He did not see that Death was looking at him angrily, lifting his hand into the air, and threatening him with his withered fist. He lifted up the sick girl and placed her head where her feet had been. Then he gave her some of the herb, and her cheeks immediately turned red, and life stirred in her once again.

Death, seeing that he had been cheated out of his property for a second time, approached the physician with long strides and said, "You are finished. Now it is your turn."

Then Death seized him so firmly with his ice-cold hand that he could not resist, and led him into an underground cavern. There the physician saw how thousands and thousands of candles were burning in endless rows, some large, others medium-sized, others small. Every instant some died out, and others were relit, so that the little flames seemed to be jumping about in constant change. "See," said Death, "these are the life-lights of mankind. The large ones belong to children, the medium-sized ones to married people in their best years, and the little ones to old people. However, even children and young people often have only a tiny candle."

"Show me my life-light," said the physician, thinking that it still would be very large. Death pointed to a little stump that was just threatening to go out, and said, "See, there it is." – "Oh, dear godfather," said the horrified physician, "light a new one for me. Do it as a favor to me, so that I can enjoy my life, and become king and the husband of the beautiful princess." – "I cannot,"

answered Death. "One must go out before a new one is lighted."
– "Then set the old one onto a new one that will go on burning
after the old one is finished," begged the physician.

Death pretended that he was going to fulfill this wish and
took hold of a large new candle; but desiring revenge, he
purposely made a mistake in relighting it, and the little piece fell
down and went out. The physician immediately fell to the
ground, and he too was now in the hands of Death.

Some Questions to Reflect Upon:

*In the story, the poor man chooses Death over God and the Devil as
the thirteenth child's godfather, because Death treats all people, no
matter their status, the same. Should all people be treated the same,
even though they might have differing needs?*

*This is a story in which the godson attempts to trick Death, which
he does when he saves the king and the king's daughter by turning
the bed. How do people now try to trick Death?*

*The godson decides to trick death in the face of power and beauty.
Does power or beauty turn your head or allow you to make decisions
that are not thought through as consequences?*

*Is Death right to seek revenge on his godson? Or is Death simply
returning the characteristic he was chosen for by the poor man –
treating all people the same even his own godson?*

A Contemporary Story

I discovered I had a fatal disease in 2004. I was diagnosed with
Berger's syndrome. IgA Nephropathy, its formal name, is an
autoimmune disease. There is genetic component to getting this
disease. For some people, like me, slowly over years the body
produces too much protein and the protein destroys the

nephrons or filtering system of the kidneys. For a few people, the condition causes kidney failure. In these cases, as mine is, dialysis and kidney transplant are the only treatment. I have been lucky and received a kidney in 2010. There are no symptoms; however, I suffered from gout for a long time as my kidney failed.

Several years earlier I had been diagnosed with another autoimmune condition: Hashimoto's Syndrome. Wikipedia reports: "Hashimoto's thyroiditis or chronic lymphocytic thyroiditis is an autoimmune disease in which the thyroid gland is attacked by a variety of cell- and antibody-mediated immune processes. It was the first disease to be recognized as an autoimmune disease. It was first described by the Japanese specialist Hakaru Hashimoto in Germany in 1912." I had a thyroidectomy in 2002. I still have the disease.

Autoimmune diseases are thought to be caused by the transfer of overactive cells from mother to fetus. Medical doctors are only recently focusing on them, and diagnosing and treating them is difficult. Only recently has the above discovery of cause been suggested and is not proved.

I have been told that an autoimmune disease is a rage of the body against the self.

The gift of a fatal disease is that it often produces a new perspective on living. For me there was no more denial of death and no longer could I feel immortal. I found myself trans-forming. I needed the energy of the Warrior to have the courage to watch my body die, to undergo the trauma of the dialysis sessions three times a week, to continue working with recovering men and women reentering the community from incarceration, and to continue to live my life as vibrantly as I could. I needed it to overcome the fear of dying. I needed it to endure the side effects of the dialysis between sessions – blood pressure drops, fainting, mental cloudiness, lower energy and muscle cramps.

I needed the energy of the Lover to deeply come into

relationship with myself, with my brother and sister dialysis patients and the staff that cared for us; with my sustaining family, especially my wife Barbara; with my community. Lover energy deepened my connection with the clients who were coming to the Council on Prevention Education: Substances (COPES, Inc.) where I worked in the aftercare program. I had to deepen my relationship with God, who I recognize as the spirit or love that stretches out across the world invisibly – the spirit of love, creation, vibrancy, prophesy, and wisdom.

I needed the energy of the Magician to continue to do my work, to figure out how I wanted my life to change and become more abundant and giving. I devised plans for writing and creating new training programs. I very much wanted to give back as I had been given to by others – mentors, teachers, supporters. The incubation of many of the ideas in this book took place during these years.

I was transforming through this traumatic and difficult time into my King energy. The gift here was immediacy. I did not have to wait and deny and pretend that someday I would die. The challenge of dying was always present. It became the catalyst for my kingship. Through this arrival at the gate of becoming an Elder, I was able to choose life, contend with death consciously, and develop an entirely new consciousness regarding life. My spirituality deepened and the suffering of the treatments became the spiritual path and practice – using the time to meditate, pray for others, consider my life, contemplate, forgive and accept. The dialysis center became my monastery, my way of living, my connection to my brothers and sisters, and the place of my conversion from egocentric Warrior to Vibrant Emeritus.

In a sense I got to experience dying from a fatal disease as I watched my body completely go down physically, mentally and emotionally until it became no longer possible for my body to function without the dialysis machine. On dialysis, life was put on hold. I was kept alive, but with the side effects, limited energy and dependence on the machine. On the day of my transplant I was given again the gift of life. Gradually over the past three years, my amazing body has recovered almost all of its energy, its functions, its ability to think and feel. Depression is less frequent. Embracing who I am and what I want to be until my next death is exhilarating.

Challenges

Challenge One: Writing Your Story

1. Reflect on the classic tale of *Godfather Death*, and think about its themes, its use of archetypes, and its perspectives on growth, change, and healing.
2. Reflect on the contemporary story and how it connects with the classic tale.
3. Reflect on your own journey so far, and write your own contemporary story and where you see yourself, and your relationship with death.

Challenge Two: Dying Visualization

1. Either read the following visualization into a recorder so that you can play it to yourself or ask a person you trust to read it to you. Make sure to pause for ten seconds between each line.
2. Place a favorite pen and notebook or journal near to where you are visualizing.
3. Playing soft, meditative music can enhance the experience.
4. Follow the direction of the visualization narrative:

I invite you to lie on the floor on your back and get comfortable. Find a place where you feel alone.

When you are ready, I invite you to close your eyes.

Take a deep cleansing breath, that is, breathe in through your nose, hold the breath and then slowly release the breath through your mouth. Let's do this together,

Take a deep breath filling your lungs for a count of 10, hold your breath for a count of 10, then release slowly for a count of 10.

Now I invite you to breathe normally, deeply, slowly, and concentrate on the breath coming in and flowing out.

As you slowly breathe in, imagine that you are allowing a deep white light to enter your head. It is beautiful, healing and relaxing light.

The light fills your body and flows into your head and out through your toes.

As you will with light, your body relaxes. You continue to breathe very deeply.

You feel your body sink into the floor.

Any tension you might hold flow out.

The healing and relaxing light flows through you through your deep breathing.

Notice where you might hold any tension and let it go.

In your neck, in your shoulders

Let it go.

In your arms and hands

Let it go

In your chest and stomach

Let it go

In your hips and thighs

Let it go

In your calves, ankles or feet

Any tension,

Let it go

Breathe deeply and let it go
As you breathe deeply you notice around you a forest
You are lying on the ground
It is a beautiful day
You look straight up and the trees seem to touch the sky
You can see a circle of sky at the tops of the trees
Your body feels safe on the ground,
Your body feels heavy but relaxed
You sink relaxed, the earth mother holding you
Breathing deeply, deeply breathing
You breathe into the fecund earth
Feeling the nourishment of the mother
The warm sun on your body, a gentle breeze flowing over you
Your hearing is heightened as you breathe in the day
The oneness of you and the forest
Gradually, you feel the presence of someone
He sits down beside you
He smiles and you feel comfortable, connected deeply
And then another person, and another
These people are closest to you,
Family, or like, to you
Each of them carries a memory from your life
With your permission, each of them blesses you
With their words, with their touch
Quietly and slowly each rises and takes leave of you
You feel deeply blessed
Another person sits next to you
This is a person you need to forgive
Or to receive forgiveness from
It is a deep and loving moment
As each of you lets go of the sadness and fear
And breathes into the love you both share
With gentle forgiveness, this person takes leave of you
You let go, let go, let go with each breath

And another sits next to you
This is the one, the one you love the most
The one who loves you the most
The one who holds your soul
And the one who will let you go
To the freedom and amazement awaiting
You breathe into this love
And all those you have loved who have loved you are present
Words come to you
Words of the legacy you will leave
Words of the gratitude you feel
Words of the love you give
You are your deepest essence
You feel yourself rising
Rising into the light that descends
From the circle of blue at the top of the trees
Essence into the essence of all that we are
Very gradually and in your own time
Remembering all you experienced
Remembering the presence of the presence within you
And knowing that today
The rest of the day you will be serene
And happy and connected to yourself
And to the others you meet and see
For you know that we are all one
And all is one
Drifting back into the room
Until you are fully back and you know
It is time to breathe deeply and open your eyes gradually
And feel the solidity of the floor beneath you
And taking a long and easy stretch you
Move into a sitting position
And stretching again look around you
Pick up your favorite pen

In your notebook or journal make notes of your experience.

Challenge Three: Afterlife?

1. Nearly every culture and religion has developed a vision of the afterlife. For the Greeks it was a pale and shadowing place, a pale imitation of the heroic life. For Christians it is the reward of reunion with God and loved ones in a heaven. *The Tibetan Book of the Dead* gives a very detailed explanation of what happens to the soul after death. Some believe that all is energy and we simply return to that energy that is the universe. Consider your own personal vision.

2. Choose a medium in which you'd like to express yourself. Using this medium express your thoughts, feelings and insights about what happens after death.

Challenge Four: Legacy

1. Meet with someone you love and trust. Or meet with several people you know will tell you the truth.

2. Take notes as you ask them what your life has meant to them – what has been your gift or legacy. Ask them to tell you what they wished and hoped for you. Ask them to tell you anything that they know about you that you seem not to know.

3. Take these notes and write a document that might be read at a memorial service.

4. Write to each of those you interviewed, thanking them and answering these same questions for them. Save these in an important place to be read at a memorial service.

A Poem to Contemplate

Thanatopsis
By William Cullen Bryant

To him who in the love of nature holds
Communion with her visible forms, she speaks
A various language; for his gayer hours
She has a voice of gladness, and a smile
And eloquence of beauty; and she glides
Into his darker musings, with a mild
And healing sympathy that steals away
Their sharpness ere he is aware. When thoughts
Of the last bitter hour come like a blight
Over thy spirit, and sad images
Of the stern agony, and shroud, and pall,
And breathless darkness, and the narrow house,
Make thee to shudder, and grow sick at heart; –
Go forth, under the open sky, and list
To Nature's teachings, while from all around –
Earth and her waters, and the depths of air –
Comes a still voice. Yet a few days, and thee
The all-beholding sun shall see no more
In all his course; nor yet in the cold ground,
Where thy pale form was laid, with many tears,
Nor in the embrace of ocean, shall exist
Thy image. Earth, that nourished thee, shall claim
Thy growth, to be resolved to earth again,
And, lost each human trace, surrendering up
Thine individual being, shalt thou go
To mix forever with the elements,
To be a brother to the insensible rock
And to the sluggish clod, which the rude swain
Turns with his share, and treads upon. The oak

Shall send his roots abroad, and pierce thy mold.

Yet not to thine eternal resting-place
Shalt thou retire alone, nor couldst thou wish
Couch more magnificent. Thou shalt lie down
With patriarchs of the infant world – with kings,
The powerful of the earth – the wise, the good,
Fair forms, and hoary seers of ages past,
All in one mighty sepulcher. The hills
Rock-ribbed and ancient as the sun, – the vales
Stretching in pensive quietness between;
The venerable woods – rivers that move
In majesty, and the complaining brooks
That make the meadows green; and, poured round all,
Old Ocean's gray and melancholy waste, –
Are but the solemn decorations all
Of the great tomb of man. The golden sun,
The planets, all the infinite host of heaven,
Are shining on the sad abodes of death
Through the still lapse of ages. All that tread
The globe are but a handful to the tribes
That slumber in its bosom. – Take the wings
Of morning, pierce the Barcan wilderness,
Or lose thyself in the continuous woods
Where rolls the Oregon, and hears no sound,
Save his own dashings – yet the dead are there:
And millions in those solitudes, since first
The flight of years began, have laid them down
In their last sleep – the dead reign there alone.

So shalt thou rest – and what if thou withdraw
In silence from the living, and no friend
Take note of thy departure? All that breathe
Will share thy destiny. The gay will laugh

When thou art gone, the solemn brood of care
Plod on, and each one as before will chase
His favorite phantom; yet all these shall leave
Their mirth and their employments, and shall come
And make their bed with thee. As the long train
Of ages glides away, the sons of men –
The youth in life's fresh spring, and he who goes
In the full strength of years, matron and maid,
The speechless babe, and the gray-headed man –
Shall one by one be gathered to thy side,
By those, who in their turn, shall follow them.

So live, that when thy summons comes to join
The innumerable caravan, which moves
To that mysterious realm, where each shall take
His chamber in the silent halls of death,
Thou go not, like the quarry-slave at night,
Scourged to his dungeon, but, sustained and soothed
By an unfaltering trust, approach thy grave
Like one who wraps the drapery of his couch
About him, and lies down to pleasant dreams.

Some Questions to Reflect Upon:

What might be your spiritual connection to Nature?

How might connection to Nature help one die consciously?

How might one's understanding of death affect one's life?

Does this poem lessen or increase one's fear of death?

Practices

1. Many great poets have offered their insights on Death. It is a universal topic. Using the Internet, search for death poems. Contemplate the poems and reflect on the insights you gain.

2. Examine the lives of saints and religious leaders who lived lives of blessing and giving. See how they died and what they said at the end of their lives.

3. Examine the 10 Concentrations Michael Gurian suggests in his book *The Wonder of Aging*. Measure how you are progressing once a month.

4. Seek out a spiritual director and discuss dying and death with him or her.

Growth Questions

What are my spiritual beliefs about God, Death and an afterlife?

How can I best accept and face death?

What do I want to be my legacy after my death?

Who must I forgive? Who might I seek forgiveness from?

Can I transform suffering into something positive?

How does the fact of death affect my view of living?

References

Angell, Cathy M. *My Spirit Flies: Portraits and Prose of Women In Their Power.* Bellingham, Washington: Bay City Press. 1997

Arrien, Angeles. *The Second Half of Life: The Blossoming of Your Creative Self.* CD set. Boulder, CO: Sounds True. 1997

Arrien, Angeles. *The Second Half of Life: Opening the Eight Gates of Wisdom.* Boulder, CO: Sounds True. 2005

Arrien, Angeles. *Signs of Life: The Five Universal Shapes and How to Use Them.* New York: Jeffery P. Tarcher. 1998

Bain, R. Nesbitt. *Russian Fairy Tales From the Skazki of Polevoi.* 2010: http://www.gutenberg.org/files/34705/34705-h/34705-h.htm#ch7

Bryant, William Cullen. *Thanatopsis.* Retrieved 4/15/14 from http://www.poetryfoundation.org/poem/180813

Bly, Robert. *Iron John: A Book About Men.* Cambridge, MA: Da Capo Press. 2004

Campbell, Joseph. *The Hero with a Thousand Faces.* Princeton, NJ: Princeton University Press. 1949

Chinen, Allan B. *Beyond the Hero: Classic Stories of Men in Search of Soul.* New York: GP Putnam's Sons. 1993

Chinen, Allan B. *In the Ever After: Fairy Tales and the Second Half of Life.* Wilmette, Illinois: Chiron Publications. 1989

Chinen, Allan B. *Once Upon a Midlife: Classic Stories and Mythic Tales to Illuminate the Middle Years.* Los Angeles: Jeremy P. Tarcher. 1992

Cohen, Gene D., MD, PhD. *The Creative Age: Awakening Human Potential in the Second Half of Life.* New York: Avon Books. 2000

Cohen, Gene D., MD, PhD. *The Mature Mind: The Positive Power of the Aging Brain.* New York: Basic Books. 2005

Eschenbach, Wolfram von. *Parzival.* New York: Penguin Books. 1980

Frost, Robert. *The Road Not Taken.* Retrieved 4/15/14 from

http://www.poetryfoundation.org/poem/173536

Frost, Robert. *Birches*. Retrieved 4/15/14 from www.poetryfoundation.org/poem/173524

Gerzon, Mark. *Coming Into Our Own: Understanding the Adult Metamorphosis*. New York: Delacorte Press. 1992

Grimm Brothers. *Godfather Death*. Retrieved 4/15/14 from http://classiclit.about.com/library/bl-etexts/grimm/bl-grimm-godfatherdeath.htm

Grimm, Brothers. *The Water of Life*. Retrieved 4/15/14 from http://www.authorama.com/grimms-fairy-tales-51.html

Jacob Grimm. *Grimm's Fairy Tales*. Gutenburg

Jacob Grimm. *Household Stories by the Brothers Grimm*. Gutenburg

Gurian, Michael. *The Wonder of Aging: A New Approach to Embracing Life After Fifty*. New York: Atria Books. 2013

Hillman, James. *The Force of Character and the Lasting Life*. New York: Random House. 1999

Hollis, James, PhD. *Finding Meaning in the Second Half of Life: How to Finally, Really Grow Up*. New York: Gotham Books. 2005

Hopkins, Gerard Manley. *God's Grandeur*. Retrieved 4/15/14 from http://www.poetryfoundation.org/poem/173660

Johnson, Robert A. and Jerry M. Ruhl, PhD. *Living Your Unlived Life: Coping with Unrealized Dreams and Fulfilling Your Purpose in the Second Half of Life*. New York: Jeremy P. Tarcher. 2007

Jones, Terry. *The Elder Within: The Source of Mature Masculinity*. Wilsonville, Oregon: BookPartners, Inc. 2001

Jung, Carl. "Psychology and Religion" (1938). In *CW 11: Psychology and Religion: West and East*. P. 131

Lang, A. *The Brown Fairy Book*. London: Longman, Green. 1914. Retrieved 4/15/14 from http://etc.usf.edu/lit2go/139/the-brown-fairy-book/4344/story-of-wali-dad-the-simple-hearted/

Leder, Drew, MD, PhD. *Spiritual Passages: Embracing Life's Sacred Journey*. New York: Jeremy P. Tarcher/Putnam. 1997

Martin, Kev. "The Myth of Parsifal."

http://kevmartin.org/samples/parsifal.html

Meade, Michael. *Men and the Water of Life: Initiation and the Tempering of Men.* San Francisco: HarperSanFrancisco. 1993

Moody, Harry R., PhD. *The Five Stages of the Soul: Charting the Spiritual Passages That Shape Our Lives.* New York: Anchor Books. 1997

Moore, Robert and Douglas Gillette. *King, Warrior, Magician, Lover: Rediscovering the Archetypes of the Mature Masculine.* New York: HarperCollins. 1990

Plotkin, Bill. *Nature and the Human Soul: Cultivating Wholeness and Community in a Fragmented World.* Novato, California: New World Library. 2008

Pound, Ezra. *In the Old Age of the Soul.* Retrieved on 4/15/14 from http://www.poemhunter.com/poem/in-the-old-age-of-the-soul/

Rohr, Richard. *Adam's Return: The Five Promises of Male Initiation.* New York: Crossroad Publishing Company. 2004

Rohr, Richard. *Falling Upward: A Spirituality for the Two Halves of Life.* San Francisco: Jossey-Bass. 2011

Rohr, Richard. *Quest for the Grail.* New York: Crossroad Publishing Company. 1994

Robinson, John C. *Bedtime Stories for Elders: What Fairy Tales Can Teach Us About the New Aging.* Washington: O-Books. 2012

Robinson, John C. *What Aging Men Want: The Odyssey as a Parable of Male Aging.* Washington: Psyche Books. 2013

Russian Fairy Tales From the Skazki of Polevoi. Gutenburg

Schachter-Shalomi, Zalman and Ronald S. Miller. *From Age-ing to Sage-ing: A Profound New Vision of Growing Older.* New York: Grand Central Publishing. 1995

Teasdale, Sara. *Wisdom.* Retrieved 4/15/14 from http://www.poemhunter.com/best-poems/sara-teasdale/wisdom-2/

Tennyson, Alfred, Lord. *Ulysses.* Retrieved 4/15/14 from http://www.poetryfoundation.org/poem/174659

Whitbourne, Susan Krauss. "The Joys of Generativity in Midlife," *Huffington Post*, 2/06/2013

Wilde, Oscar. *The Picture of Dorian Gray*. Retrieved 4/15/14 from http://www.onreadz.com/book/The-Picture-of-Dorian-Gray-1486716

Wordsworth, William. *Lines Composed a Few Miles above Tintern Abbey, On Revisiting the Banks of the Wye during a Tour. July 13, 1798.* Retrieved 4/15/14 from http://www.poetryfoundation.org/poem/174796

Yolen, Jane, ed. *Gray Heroes: Elder Tales from Around the World*. New York: Penguin Press. 1999

Websites

http://www.johnrobinson.org/works.htm

http://www.mosaicvoices.org/

www.pitt.edu/~dash/aging.html#stages

http://www.jewishsacredaging.com/

http://poeticsofaging.org/

http://www.secondjourney.org

http://www.storydoctor.net/

About the Author

Ric Stuecker is a nationally recognized author, trainer, and coach in the areas of conscious aging, initiation, personal empowerment, and positive youth development. He is co-founder of the Vibrant Emeritus Center. A professional facilitator and coach, he has worked with communities, school districts, businesses, and individuals throughout the United States to discover their mission and strategies that reflect a passion to effect positive change. He has developed powerful, life-changing experiences for both youth and adults including the Vibrant Emeritus Initiation.

The Vibrant Emeritus Center presents life-changing experiences for men and women 50 years and older who embrace the second half of their lives as Vibrant Emeriti. The Center is a collaborative of nationally known authors, presenters, facilitators, trainers, storytellers, folklorists, body healers, poets and program developers. Annually, the Center presents the Vibrant Emeritus Initiation for men over 50 on the first weekends of June and December. For more information, go to www.vibrantemeritus. com or e-mail Ric at asunbear123@gmail.com.

Ric lives in Louisville, Kentucky with his wife, Barbara. They have two grandchildren living close by and two living in Asheville, North Carolina.

BOOKS

O is a symbol of the world, of oneness and unity. In different cultures it also means the "eye," symbolizing knowledge and insight. We aim to publish books that are accessible, constructive and that challenge accepted opinion, both that of academia and the "moral majority."

Our books are available in all good English language bookstores worldwide. If you don't see the book on the shelves ask the bookstore to order it for you, quoting the ISBN number and title. Alternatively you can order online (all major online retail sites carry our titles) or contact the distributor in the relevant country, listed on the copyright page.

See our website www.o-books.com for a full list of over 500 titles, growing by 100 a year.

And tune in to myspiritradio.com for our book review radio show, hosted by June-Elleni Laine, where you can listen to the authors discussing their books.

mySpiritRadio